This book is dedicated to all
beings interested in optimal health, weight,
and the well-being of our planet.

Special Thanks to Randall Fitzgerald, Susan Maharaj, Vivify Agency,
and all of our colleagues and friends who have contributed to all the
successful work that we have achieved at Hippocrates Wellness since 1956.

*Although referenced in several studies, we do not support animal testing.

Forewords	06

Introduction: Make Healthy Weight a Lifestyle Choice

What Is Your Contribution to Weight Gain Trends?	15
We Began Fighting Fat Decades Ago	17
Our Comprehensive Synergistic Solution	21

Part One: Hidden Ways You Attract Body Fat

Soil Micronutrient Depletion Spurs Weight Gain	24
Your Stage of Life Influences Weight Gain	28
Aging Disrupts Your Hormones & Adds Pounds	30
Short and Long Sleep Duration Promotes Obesity	32
Chronic Stress Influences Your Weight	35
Your Cell Phone May Play a Role	38
Insulin Resistance Triggers Weight Gain	40
Mix Stress with Toxins, You Get Fatter	42
Beware of These Serious Chemical Offenders	45
Three Categories of Products Give Chemical Exposure	48
Don't Overlook the Impact of Your Medications	51
Hidden Triggers for Food Cravings	53
Food Advertising Makes You Eat More	56
Diet Products Can Cause Weight Gain	58
Addiction Tricks of Food Manufacturers	60
Highlights of Part One	63

Part Two: Why Diets Usually Fail You

Rounding Up the Usual Diet Program Suspects	67
25 Diets Contrasted	67
Atkins Diet	67
Bahamian Diet	68
DASH (Dietary Approaches to Stop Hypertension) Diet	68
Eco-Atkins Diet	69
Fasting	69
GOLO Diet	70
Jenny Craig	70
Keto Diet	71
Macrobiotic Diet	72
Mediterranean Diet	72
Noom	73
Nordic Diet	73
Nutrisystem Diet	74
Ornish Diet	74
Paleo Diet	75
Raw Food Diet	76
SlimFast Diet	77
South Beach Diet	77
Therapeutic Lifestyle Changes Diet	78
Vegan Diet	79
Vegetarian Diet	80
Volumetric Diet	81
Wild Diet	81
WW Diet (formerly Weight Watchers)	82
Zone Diet	82
Revisiting Weight Loss Among Popular Diets	83
Popular Diets Are Micronutrient Deficient	86
Why a Vegan Diet Equals Weight Loss	88
How Safe and Affordable Are Weight Loss Drugs?	90
Challenging Weight Loss Supplement Purity	93
Why Exercise Fails to Keep Excess Weight Off	95
What Happens to Fat Cells When You Lose Pounds?	98
Combinations of Factors that Keep the Weight Off	99
Highlights of Part Two	101

Part Three: Proven Strategies for Self-Healing

Mind Strength for Weight Health	**103**
Train Your Brain to Resist Weight Gain	103
Does Your Stomach Control Your Food Choices?	105
Learn to Delay Gratification	108
Distract Yourself from Cravings	110
Try Acceptance, Not Suppression	112
'Surf' Your Urges	114
The Biggest Craving of All Is Chocolate	117
'Tap Away' Cravings	120
Mental Imagery & Sounds Can Assist You	121
Visualization to Focus Your Mind	123
Use Mind Relaxation for Weight Loss	126
Experiment with Behavioral Change Technology	128
Action Tip: Breathwalk Away from Cravings	130
Action Tip: Dissolve Your Toxic Urges	132
Action Tip: Distance Yourself from the Craving	133
Action Tip: Visualize Your Weight Goals	134
Food Choices for Weight Health	**136**
Distracted Eating Invites Obesity	136
Eat Too Fast, Gain More Weight	138
Time Your Food Intake for Weight Loss	139
Turn Down Your Stress Eating Dial	141
Transform 'Emotional Eating' into 'Intuitive Eating'	142
Thirteen Fat Fighting Foods & Nutrients	143
Plant-Based Supplements Melt Abdominal Fat	150
End Cravings Using Spinach, Peppers & Cinnamon	152
Action Tip: Put Your Focus on Food Quality	154
Action Tip: Mindful Eating for Weight Control	155
Action Tip: Turn Meal Choices into a Health Ritual	156
Body Tune-Ups for Weight Health	**157**
Super Immunity for Weight Control	157
How Your Diet & Gut Microbes Interact	160
Don't Overlook the Importance of Phytochemicals	164
Reverse Insulin Resistance	166
Post-Meal Strolls Control Blood Sugar	167
Put Your Hormones Back in Balance	169
Body Fat Reduction with Freezing	173
Regular Cold Exposure Can Help Burn Fat	177
Saunas Can Melt Away Pounds	179
Lose Weight While You Sleep	181
How Many Daily Steps Do You Need?	182
When You Exercise Does Matter	183
Action Tip: Feeling Good Vibrations	184
Action Tip: 'Power Naps' to Burn Calories	185
Action Tip: Burn Fat by Exercising Before Breakfast	186
Lifestyle Rituals for Weight Health	**187**
Combine Healthy Habits to Amplify Effects	187
Make Exercise a Lifestyle Choice	189
Beware of Sabotaging Behaviors	192
Create Your Own Weight Management Plan	194
Our Hippocrates Self-Healing Weight Program	198
Action Tip: Our Program Guidelines for Healthy Weight	200
Your Diet Choices Carry Climate Consequences	201
Highlights of Part Three	205
About the Authors	207

Forewords
Three Generations
of Praise

BY DR ZACH BUSH MD
& DR T. COLIN CAMPBELL, PHD
& DR BERNIE SIEGEL MD

Documents Our Divorce From Nature's Nutrition

You have picked up this book for a reason. You are compelled to understand the underpinnings of the loss of vitality of modern humanity. Perhaps it is fatigue, weight gain, chronic pain, diabetes, or autoimmune disease in your own journey or the journey of your clients as a health care provider.

Regardless of the reason, you are reaching into the root cause of the chronic disease epidemic that has become the defining feature of the modern Homo sapien sapien.

As a seeming capstone on a history of 200,000 years of human biology, we have suddenly created the widespread collapse of human cellular metabolism in the few short decades that closed the second millennium of the extractive machine of Western Colonialism. Interestingly, at the root of this extinction-level threat to human health is the very technological system that allowed for the nearly inexorable expansion of Western civilization: the modern food system. With the advent of commercial food production in Europe and North Africa 2000 years ago, we began a long steady divorce from the source of life - soil. The alchemical transformation of the atomic physics building blocks of the mere 92 elements of the periodic chart into the extraordinary bounty of beauty and life-giving nutrients composed by the vast plant kingdom.

What extreme biodiversity and beauty we can taste on this planet. Seeds, flowers, nuts, fruits, vegetables, and mushrooms. The animals of planet earth can choose from a stunning, exquisite variety of foods that stimulate all the senses to induce a state of pleasure that enriches the experience of the life made possible by the nutrients within. In our capacity to appreciate this beautiful bounty of botany, we have become an extraordinary pollinator species for life to spread its beauty faster across the planet.

We have carried botanical specimens into every niche of the ecosystem; we have patiently bred new varieties of species over hundreds of generations of curious farmers and food scientists. How did we lose our relationship with our food? No matter how much we eat now, there is a paucity of life. The energy and nutrients within our food web have collapsed.

Perhaps by a stroke of grace, our scientific advancements have paralleled the widespread collapse of metabolism to give us the revelation of how we have broken our relationship with our food and a path forward to re-engaging our nature to heal. Over the last three decades, the science of genomics has come of age to reveal the intricate and critical relationship between human health and the extraordinary microscopic ecosystems (bacteria, fungi, protozoa) that constitute the soils of the earth that produce our food and the human intestinal soil that make available food nutrients to your 70 trillion human cells, as well as the caloric energy to the 14 quadrillion microbes that live within the human cells – the mitochondria. The conclusion of these decades of research is this: to be a healthy, vital human, we must embody a vast ecosystem of species that cooperatively co-create extreme energetic and creative capacity of biology and all living systems.

So here you are, with a book in your hand, ready to delve into the revelations of cause and effect of our divorce from nature's nutrition. You are your own pioneer wading into the exploration for a path back into nature to find healing and vitality. It is not just your health that hangs in the balance of your efforts, but that of our species and the millions of others that compose the beauty of life on earth. It is time to reconnect, so indulge yourself in this self-healing diet journey. Bon appetite.

- Dr Zach Bush MD, Creator of The Journey of Intrinsic Health

A Self-Healing Program for Everyone

Brian Clement and Anna Maria Clement are among the earliest contributors I know who began the present-day discussion of the benefits of a non-traditional and nutrient-dependent medical practice. They are best known as the co-directors of Hippocrates Wellness (formerly the Hippocrates Health Institute) located in West Palm Beach, Florida. Many people have attended their clinic with considerable success and I have presented several lectures there, enabling me to spend time with Brian and Anna Maria sharing our ideas on nutrition and health.

As an experimental researcher in the fields of nutrition and biochemistry for many decades, my views have been shaped by a large body of empirical findings that demonstrate how the nutrients in what we eat can either keep us healthy, or else their absence can cause illness and disease. The Clements have discovered this truth firsthand with their thousands of guests at Hippocrates, who suffered from every imaginable ailment. By using an organic living foods diet they were able to strengthen their immune system, while taking off excess pounds and creating a healthy body weight.

I am impressed with the significant body of evidence that points to the superior health value of raw foods, as recommended and practiced by the Hippocrates program. The production of toxins during the cooking of certain foods, the worrisome residues of noxious chemical contaminants in food, and the destruction and loss of important nutrients during cooking are all well documented.

My own research has shown the broad and profound nutritional activities of whole plant-based foods (vegetables, fruits and cereal grains). I emphasize the 'wholeness' characteristic of food to refer to those foods found in nature during most of our evolutionary history, which have fashioned our biological responses to food. The added benefit is that such a nutrient-dense diet helps humans to maintain a healthy body weight.

I feel comfortable recommending this book because I have seen how Brian and Anna Maria have substantial real-life experience and evidence to support the Hippocrates health and self-healing protocols. There may be no better message for human health than this one!

-T. Colin Campbell, Ph.D., *professor of nutritional biochemistry at Cornell University, is the author of the international bestseller,* The China Study.

You Will Watch Your Body Heal and Change

This book is a gift and a resource for anyone dealing with obesity. It truly guides you with both information and inspiration. I have learned, as this book will also reveal, information alone is not the solution to all our problems, be they emotional or physical. We need inspiration and not just information. It all begins with our childhood experience, self-esteem, and love. Parenting is a very misunderstood aspect of health and healing in our life.

If you were abused as a child and grew up without feeling loved, why not reward yourself with food, drugs, alcohol, and other addictions? I have learned about these from my work with cancer patients. You cannot separate your health, lifestyle, and experience.

I hope with this book and my words of experience and guidance, you will find your way to health and healing. The book discusses diet and lifestyle, and treatment, but you are the solution when you educate yourself and follow the path to healing in your life and not the one to self-abuse and punishment as a way of repaying yourself for all your difficulties.

So do what makes you happy by reading this book and following its wisdom by seeing them as God's redirections and a way to contribute to everyone who is in need.

There is information available here to be joined with your inspiration and create the result you desire. The quick fix may not last because it does not represent a real change in you. A diet can be like chemotherapy with many side effects, or it can be a gift with no problems or side effects because it is your choice, and your body does not react in a negative way to your change.

You can reparent yourself and care for your inner child in the way it deserves. Think of a word that describes how you feel about being obese. Now ask yourself what else in your life fits that word you selected and eliminate everything in your life that fits that word and watch how your life changes and your problems fade away. When you love your inner child, you will find self-control and self-love, your life will heal, and so will your body. Remember, information and inspiration are two separate entities.

When you love yourself, self-control is not an issue. So put up pictures and your drawings of yourself and love that kid. The colors you use and the image you create of yourself will tell you a lot and help you to heal. With self-love, your body chemistry changes, and self-induced healing of your problem can be accomplished. Food is not love, but it can nourish you so that you love yourself, your body, and your life. When you love yourself and life, you don't need advice on how to live a long healthy life because it becomes you and your life.

So start loving yourself and not just the things you eat. Love will nourish you in many ways. And remember to find the word that describes how it feels to be obese, remove whatever it represents in your life, and watch your body heal and change.

- Dr Bernie Siegel MD, Author of Love, Medicine & Miracles and The Art of Healing

INTRODUCTION:

Make Healthy Weight a Lifestyle Choice

Imagine a future just a decade from now in which, as if in a science fiction horror movie, nearly everyone on the planet is obese and that condition has been normalized. (If you've seen WALL-E, the Disney animated film in which humans have degenerated into fat lazy slobs, then you get the picture.) Now imagine a future for humanity in which having a healthy weight is the norm, which is what this book is intended to help bring about.

The large majority of us live in the land of plenty…and now, in the U.S. and elsewhere, it shows in our bulging waistlines and in our rapidly declining overall health. While we don't want to needlessly alarm you or bore you with statistics, we feel an obligation to present the facts and our analysis of options in such a way as to impress upon you how truly serious our health situation has become.

We are not exaggerating when we report there is a distinct possibility that virtually the entire population of the U.S. will become overweight or obese within our own lifetimes. Though that may sound improbable, public health experts insist that if current weight-gain trends continue, this depressing scenario will come true by the year 2030, when 86% of all U.S. adults will be overweight or obese.

Even more disturbing, a team of scientists at the Johns Hopkins School of Public Health, projecting from current trends, concluded that by the year 2048, EVERY American adult will be overweight or obese, creating health conditions that will absorb most of the nation's expenditures on healthcare. These experts warn this grim future will happen unless "timely, dramatic, and effective corrective programs and policies are implemented."

We believe this book represents the "timely, dramatic and effective corrective program" necessary to avoid this grim prediction.

The evidence on which these projections are based is quite well-documented and compelling. When U.S. government health agencies began compiling average weight statistics for adults in 1960-62, an estimated 13.4% of adults in the U.S. were classified as obese. That percentage remained virtually unchanged for two decades, until the period 1988-1994 when suddenly it almost doubled to 23.2% of adults being categorized as obese. Another decade passed and adult obesity further spiked to 32.9%, a percentage increase that spanned all ethnic groups except for Asian Americans, whose increase was more modest.

Wang Y. Et al."Will all Americans become overweight or obese? Estimating the progression and cost of the US obesity epidemic." Obesity. 2012 September. "Prevalence of Overweight, Obesity, and Severe Obesity Among Adults Aged 20 and Over: United States, 1960-1962 Through 2015-2016." National Center for Health Statistics. www.cdc.gov/nchs/data/hestat/obesity_adult_15_16/obesity_adult_15_16.htm

What happened between 1988 and 2004? Could American dietary and exercise habits have rapidly and fundamentally changed in such a remarkably short period? One explanation offered by psychologists, writing in a clinical psychology journal, got bluntly to the point:

> "The marked increase (in obesity) appears to be attributable to a toxic environment that implicitly discourages physical activity while explicitly encouraging the consumption of supersized portions of high-fat, high-sugar foods."

Our contention in this book is that the 'toxic environment' around us is responsible for helping to accelerate weight gain, is quite real and a rapidly growing phenomenon and involves the spread of synthetic chemical toxicity. Part of it is largely attributable to a food industry that introduces addictive chemicals into processed foods to raise profits, while ignoring the wide-ranging impacts on human health. More on that issue later.

Let's dig into a few of the details about what our culture is experiencing.

"Obesity: responding to the global epidemic." Wadden TA. Et al. J Consult Clin Psychol. 2002 June.

What Is Your Contribution to Weight Gain Trends?

The percentage of U.S. obese adults in 2016 enduring obesity was 39.8%, and 71.6% were overweight, a percentage that includes the obese. *Imagine that, nearly three out of every four people in the U.S. carry around unhealthy excess weight.* (Overweight is defined as having a body mass index (BMI) greater than 25, while obesity is a BMI greater than 30.)

That same year, 13.9% of children aged 2-5 years of age were documented as obese, 18.4% of children 6-11 years were obese, and 20.6% of adolescents aged 12-19 years.

To illustrate how jaw-droppingly fast these percentages are rising, just two years earlier, in 2014, the adult obesity figure had been estimated at 37.9% (jumping two percentage points to 39.8% only 24 months later); the 2-5 years age group of children endured a 9.4% obesity level (jumping four and a half percentage points to 13.9% only 24 months later.)

All industrialized societies are caught in the grip of this frightening pattern.

Since 1975, worldwide obesity has almost tripled, now affecting 650 million people, with 1.9 billion adults considered overweight. That means about 39% of all adults 18 years and older on the planet are overweight, and 13% of all human adults are now obese.

For the first time in recorded human history, being overweight kills more people than being underweight. The World Health Organization reports how having a larger than normal BMI greatly raises a person's risk for getting cardiovascular disease (including heart attack and stroke), diabetes, musculoskeletal disorders, and these cancers: endometrial, breast, ovarian, prostate, liver, gallbladder, kidney and colon.

Obesity has become the number one destroyer of humankind's health.

Whether you are overweight or not, this epidemic is impacting you and your offspring in more ways than you know, as this book will document. For example, as fat accumulates in the human body, it attracts and absorbs toxic synthetic chemicals, heavy metals, and other noxious waste products from the environment. This confuses the body's cellular processes and as a result, further accelerates the weight gain process. Yet another reason why those who possess excess weight are usually the sickest among us.

"Obesity and overweight: Key Facts." World Health Organization. Feb. 16, 2018. www.who.int/news-room/fact-sheets/detail/obesity-and-overweight

We Began Fighting Fat Decades Ago

As a teenager, between the ages of 16 and 19, I (Brian) became a pioneer in American obesity after being encouraged by my loving and supportive family to continue to eat and grow. I perceived verbally that becoming bigger meant becoming stronger. A mindset that seduced me into thinking it was perfectly fine to put on those extra pounds.

Well on my way to disease and premature death, I was, fortunately, just aware enough to recognize that it wasn't normal for me to be panting as I walked upstairs. This provoked a much-needed lifestyle change to a plant-based diet which, now that I am over 70 has made me stronger, thinner, healthier and happier than I was at 20 years of age.

By contrast, I (Anna Maria) grew up in the hills on the Baltic Sea, not far from Stockholm, Sweden, and walked or cross-country skied many kilometers every day, which kept me fit despite my horribly bad northern European diet. My dad, who seemed one step above the mix, came home one day when I was 15, threw out all of the junk food from our cabinets and refrigerator, and announced that we were going to embrace a plant-based diet. I dropped a few kilos on that diet, but just as importantly, my energy level quadrupled.

That experience inspired me to work in the field of natural healthcare and for the last 50 years, it has become increasingly clear to me why the greatest worldwide disease today is that of obesity and excess weight. When I first arrived in America from Europe, I was stunned at how many large overweight people I saw, because at that time, my part of the world had only a spattering of such problems. That is unfortunately no longer the case. Today, most European countries rival the United States in the poundage problem.

Together, as a couple, working with our highly trained medical staff, we have turned Hippocrates Wellness into one of the world's premier destinations for regaining health while losing weight and promoting self-healing. In the process, among our thousands of Hippocrates guests over the years, we have seen what works and what doesn't in the quest for achieving and maintaining a healthy weight and lifestyle.

In the 1980s, renowned comedian and social activist Dick Gregory called me (Brian) asking if Hippocrates and I would help him with a new charitable project in the Bahamas. "We want to help some fat people, like I was, get skinny," he explained.

Never one to do anything in a small or inconsequential way, Gregory chose a person for us to work with who weighed at least 1,000 pounds, and must have been one of the heaviest people on the planet. This young man had literally sat in his New York City apartment for many years doing nothing but eating and gaining weight. He could no longer walk, and just getting him on a gurney and into an airplane for the flight to the Bahamas was a huge challenge.

Once there, we put the young man on our plant-based diet, using a green powder made from sprouts, algae, and other ingredients to accelerate his metabolism. (This was the same formula Gregory used with boxer Muhammed Ali during his training for two heavyweight championship bouts.) We also waded the obese man in the ocean every day for several hours, the buoyancy in the water helping to give him the exercise he needed. There was no question in my mind that it was a safe and incredibly effective method for weight loss, so we sent other morbidly obese patients through the program.

A year after this young man went on our diet, he weighed less than 300 pounds. These extraordinary results occurred several decades before the creation of popular television shows like NBC's *The Biggest Loser,* ABC's *Extreme Weight Loss*, A&E's *From Fit to Fat to Fit*, and MTV's *I Used to be Fat.*

In those early days, during our initial experiment with extreme weight loss, we gained a valuable lesson that the producers of these reality television shows would eventually discover as well - taking the weight off is usually a short-term fix unless an entire support structure is in place to ensure weight maintenance. In our client's case, he returned to his old circumstances in New York City, and when his girlfriend abruptly left him, he went back to his pattern of self-destructive eating behaviors, largely because he wasn't surrounded with sufficient psychological support. He ate his way back up to 750 pounds, at this point his heart failed him and he had to be buried in a Steinway piano container.

This sad experience gave us extraordinary insights into the pivotal role that self-loathing and unresolved personal issues play in driving destructive eating. Even more evidence came our way during this period as we interviewed guests at Hippocrates about their weight challenges. I will never forget one unusually self-reflective guest's response when I asked why she was 200 pounds overweight. She confessed that it was a way to protect herself from the hurt, sadness, and fear she had carried with her from childhood abuse.

These sorts of stories triggered a real awakening for us at Hippocrates, because her case and others demonstrated how easily unresolved personal issues can undermine any weight loss program, no matter how disciplined and determined the person might be to lose and keep off the extra pounds. **Sad people do bad things to themselves, and 'comfort eating' can be their attempt to bury emotional pain and traumas in layers of 'protective' body fat.**

Your roadblocks to the highway of fulfillment are often the unresolved issues from your past journeys. These emulsifiers of spirit need to be recognized and dealt with if healthy weight maintenance is to be achieved. That's why we emphasize incorporating counseling and behavioral change modification techniques into any sustained weight loss program to help assure its success.

Weight loss used to be a straightforward process, or so most of us were educated to believe when growing up. All you needed to do was eat less and exercise more, because, said the so-called 'experts,' gaining and losing weight was just a balancing act between burning too few calories and consuming too many calories. **From years of experience and observation, we know that humans and their weight challenges are much more complex than the fad diet programs want you to believe.**

Over the past two decades, medical science researchers have peeled back the layers of an interplay between a web of factors influencing weight gain and weight loss, including nutritional, genetic, biochemical, exercise and physiological components that either assist or foil, efforts to keep excess pounds off at the various stages of life. We have studied this interplay of factors and feel confident we have perfected a weight loss strategy using a synergy of elements that is both safe and effective, built around a self-healing diet.

Our Comprehensive Synergistic Solution

Are you losing control of your body, or do you fear you soon will? Do you no longer recognize yourself when you look in the mirror? Would you like to improve your chances of success in achieving your weight loss goals and avoid a lifetime of health problems?

The most proven weight maintenance strategy in the history of humankind is a living-foods, plant-based diet. People who have attended our Hippocrates Wellness program over the decades to optimize their immune systems while fighting cancer and other diseases always lost weight as a side effect. As word of the weight loss benefits spread, we attracted an even larger and more diverse clientele including, most recently, celebrities such as Academy Award winning actor Anthony Hopkins, Saturday Night Live comedian Colin Quinn, and Australian actress Rebel Wilson.

Our goal in this book is to help you maintain a healthy weight using our scientifically validated approach, with the added value that you reduce your risk of disease, enhance your quality of life, and lengthen your lifespan. We know the importance of taking into account all of the factors necessary for an integrated and successful weight maintenance plan, supporting your physical, psychological, social and even spiritual dimensions of health.

We explain the weight gain role played by sleep deprivation, low estrogen and testosterone ratios, stress and high cortisol levels, and the toxic effects of endocrine-disrupting chemicals found in everyday foods and consumer products. We reveal why most attempts to lose weight fail and show you what science-based research says will and won't work when you go on a diet. You will learn why you previously failed at your diet, or why your diet failed you, and how to avoid diet traps in the future. Equally important, we will help you transform your goal of maintaining a healthy weight into a practical and effective lifestyle by healing your chronic self-sabotaging attitudes, habits, and behaviors.

If you want to shed those extra pounds and keep them off, if you want to protect yourself against common diseases or even reverse them, if you want optimal health and to create a longer, more productive life, you can't afford NOT to read this self- healing book and take its information to heart.

PART ONE:

Hidden Ways You Attract Body Fat

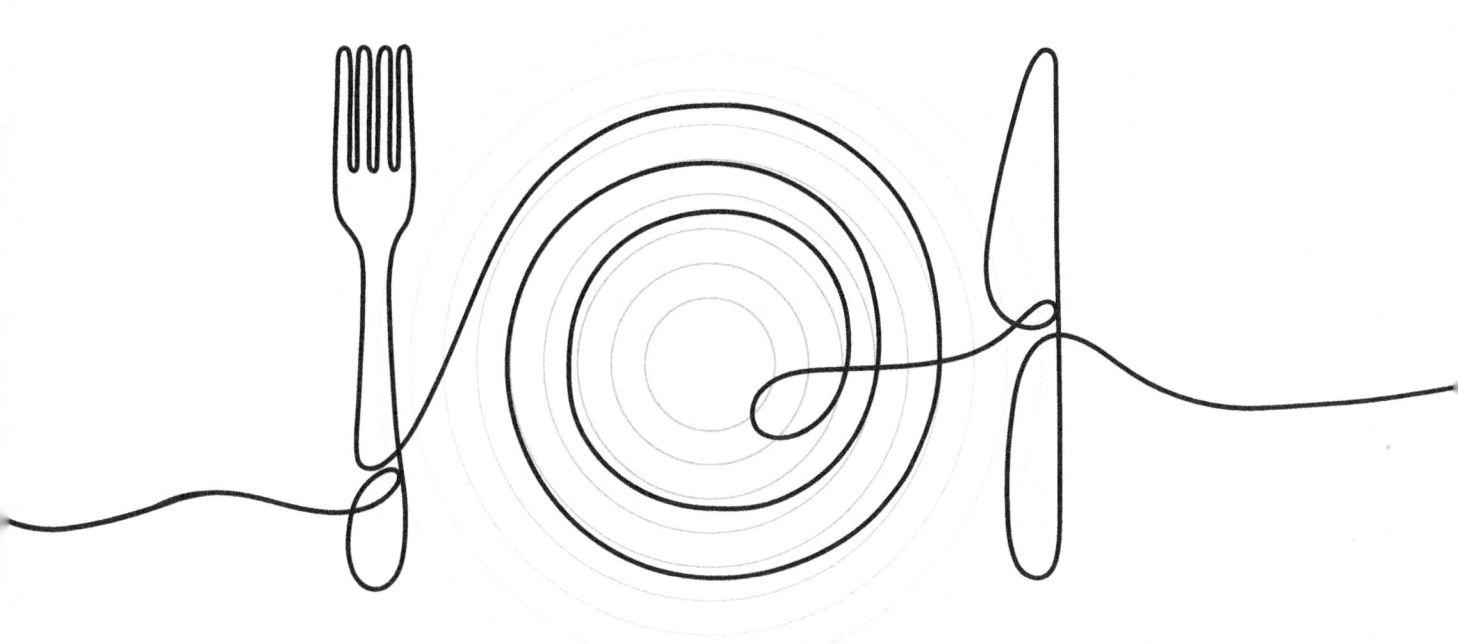

Soil Micronutrient Depletion Spurs Weight Gain

Like most of us, you probably grew up being told you must eat generous helpings of fruits and vegetables to get the nutrients you need for maintaining good overall health and a normal body weight. That was certainly sound advice…if you received it in the 1950s and 60s. Today, we face a totally different set of circumstances that undermine the value of that advice and helps to explain why so many people are gaining weight, unnecessarily degrading their health, and even losing their lives.

What both mainstream medicine practitioners and conventional nutritionists continue to ignore is something that most people still take for granted - the quality of our crop-growing soils, which determine the nutritional benefits of our fruits and vegetables.

The first major alarm about declining nutrients in soil was raised in 1992, when the United Nations Conference on Environment and Development issued a report showing huge declines "in the mineral values in farms and range soils throughout the world." Over a century, soil mineral depletions were estimated at 85% for North America, 76% for South America, 72% for Europe, and 76% for Asia. Most of this mineral depletion was due to the applications of synthetic chemical fertilizers and the effects of acid rain triggered by air pollutants.

Food scientists, writing in the *British Food Journal*, in 1997, documented significant losses of magnesium, calcium and copper in British vegetable crops. A study done in the U.S., analyzing 43 garden crops - from asparagus and broccoli to tomatoes and turnips - using U.S. Department of Agriculture yearly monitoring data between 1950 and 1999, revealed widespread nutrient declines,

"The Rio Earth Summit: Summary of the United Nations Conference on Environment and Development." November 1992.
Mayer AM. "Historical Changes in the Mineral Content of Fruits and Vegetables." British Food Journal. 1997.

particularly in vitamin C, iron, riboflavin, potassium and calcium. We are seeing "an alarming decline in food quality in 12 common vegetables," wrote the study authors.

"Some 40% of soil used for agriculture around the world is classed as either degraded or seriously degraded," reported Professor John Crawford, a biologist with the University of Sydney, in 2012.

"Because of various farming methods that strip the soil of carbon and make it less robust as well as weaker in nutrients, soil is being lost at between 10 and 40 times the rate at which it can be naturally replenished."

"Crop breeding is exacerbating this situation," continued Crawford. "Modern wheat varieties, for example, have half the micronutrients of older strains, and it's pretty much the same for fruit and vegetables." As a result, deficiencies in nutrients such as iron are helping to drive the chronic obesity levels we see in many countries.

> "Micronutrient deficiencies in our crops increasingly occur as a consequence of climate change, particularly from carbon dioxide emissions which impact nutrient formation and availability in soils."

Numerous scientific studies have documented how these micronutrient deficiencies are showing up in human bodies. A 2015 worldwide survey, for example, described how blood testing detected "widespread global micronutrient deficiencies," particularly in iron, iodine, folate, vitamin A and zinc. These shortages now "persist over generations and the intergenerational consequences we are only beginning to understand."

You may be wondering how does nutrient depletion in soils and then in your body play a role in weight gain and obesity. It's all connected to your body's metabolism. This process your body uses to tap into the nutrients from the food you eat, giving you energy to function each day, can either be stimulated or slowed down depending on the quantity and quality of the nutrients you absorb. If your metabolism slows down, of course, as a result of insufficient vitamins and minerals, *you*

Davis DR. Et al. "Changes in USDA Food Composition Data for 43 Garden Crops, 1950-1999." Journal of American College of Nutrition. 2004.
"What If the World's Soil Runs Out?" John Crawford, World Economic Forum. Dec. 14, 2012.
"Potential Effects of Climate Change on Soil Properties: A Review. Karmakar R. Et al. Science International. 2016.
Bailey RL. Et al. "The epidemiology of global micronutrient deficiencies." Ann Nutr Metab. 2015.

begin to gain weight because you are no longer burning enough calories.

It may not be a coincidence (and we don't believe it is) that the cycle of weight gain we have seen in most countries over the past half-century mirrors the cycle of mineral depletion from soils documented over the same period! **The five nutrients considered most essential for maintaining the health of your metabolism - B vitamins, Vitamin D, Iron, Calcium, and Magnesium - are among the nutrients most leached from crop soils by farming practices and climate change.**

Zinc is still another mineral nutrient whose growing absence from soils is being felt in our metabolism health. As pointed out in a 2012 report, from the Minister of Agriculture in the Netherlands, "micronutrient deficiencies in the soil can result from over fertilization with phosphate,"…which "can restrict the availability of zinc"…and that in turn can cause zinc deficiency in humans resulting "in a multiplicity of metabolic disturbances," and that includes obesity.

What are our options at both the societal and individual levels?

"Agriculture must change in ways that will closely link food production to human health and nutritional requirements," concluded Ross M. Welch, a crop specialist at the U.S. Plant, Soil and Nutrition Laboratory at Cornell University. "Because the magnitude of the problem is so great, we must use every tool at our disposal…"

Chen Y. Et al. "Importance of Nutrients and Nutrient Metabolism on Human Health." Yale J Biol Med. 2018 June. And, "Vitamins and minerals that boost metabolism." Cathleen Crichton-Stuart. Medical News Today. January 14, 2019.
Udo de Haes H. Et al. "Scarcity of micronutrients in soil, feed, food, and mineral reserves." Dutch Platform for Agriculture, Innovation & Society. September 2012. http://www.iatp.org/files/scarcity_of_micronutrients.pdf. Welch RM. "The impact of mineral nutrients in food crops on global human health." Plant and Soil. 2002.

Until adequate nutrient replenishment of our soils can occur, or until climate change stops and is no longer an issue for humanity, we may need to rely on nutritional supplements to help protect our metabolism and prevent weight gain. But since the obesity problem is complex, our solutions need to be multi-faceted and integrative, to take into account all of the extenuating circumstances in a person's life.

In this section of the book, we examine a range of other factors which could be contributing to your weight gain and your inability to take the weight off. These often-unrecognized factors include exposure to hormone-disrupting chemicals, sleep deprivation, high cortisol levels from stress, low testosterone or estrogen levels, and the abnormal stimulation of food cravings by advertising campaigns and the insertion of addictive substances into processed foods.

Your Stage of Life Influences Weight Gain

At every stage of our life, we encounter circumstances that generate opportunities for substantial weight gain. From being in the womb to entering college, from motherhood to menopause (and andropause for men), life creates vulnerable periods to trigger the development of unwanted pounds.

Let's start with the programming of how we begin life. If your mother experienced chronic stress while she was pregnant with you or when you were an infant, your risk for developing obesity later in life dramatically increases.

Using 89 pairs of twins as a study sample, scientists found in 2016 that high levels of stress in mothers dysregulated cortisol and other coping mechanisms in their children, causing anxious behaviors in the kids. Related research confirmed this anxiety helped produce overeating and weight gain in later years.

Most mothers know how the aftermath of pregnancy becomes a life stage that is often characterized by substantial weight gain that proves challenging to lose. To underscore how common this phenomenon has become, a team of scientists from a half-dozen U.S. universities assessed 774 women and their weight before, during, and 12 months after their pregnancy. "Women gained a mean of 32 pounds while pregnant," the researchers reported, and "approximately 75% of women were heavier 1-year postpartum than they were pre- pregnancy, including 47.4% retaining more than 10 lbs and 24.2% more than 20 lbs.

Brooker RJ. Et al. "Maternal negative affect during infancy is linked to disrupted patterns of diurnal cortisol and alpha asymmetry across contexts during childhood." J Exp Child Psychol. 2016 February.

Of the women with normal pre-pregnancy BMI {Body Mass Index} *one-third became overweight or obese 1 year postpartum."*

When children become young adults, and if they enter their first year of college, another weight gain stage of life kicks in, a phenomenon called 'Freshman 15.' This refers to studies done since 1985, showing that first-year college students gain an average of 15 pounds as a result of academic stress and a change in lifestyle that involves alcohol consumption and unhealthy eating. A 2015 study, published in the science journal, BMC Obesity, estimated that among 300 freshmen studied, 60.9% gained at least 7.5 pounds their first year. This was true for both male and female students.

Other life transitions typically providing triggers for weight accumulations range from marriage (especially if it becomes tumultuous) to divorce (when either sudden weight gain or weight loss can occur), to a change in habits, such as quitting smoking (which we highly recommend) but which can result in weight gain if not managed properly. All of this pales in comparison to the long-term impact and importance of a life transition that most people cannot avoid---aging and the resulting menopause symptoms for women and andropause symptoms for men.

Endres LK. Et al. "Postpartum weight retention risk factors and relationship to obesity at 1 year." Obstet Gynecol. 2015 January.
Vadeboncoeur C. Et al. "A meta-analysis of weight gain in first year university students; is freshman 15 a myth?" BMC Obesity. 2015 May.

Aging Disrupts Your Hormones & Adds Pounds

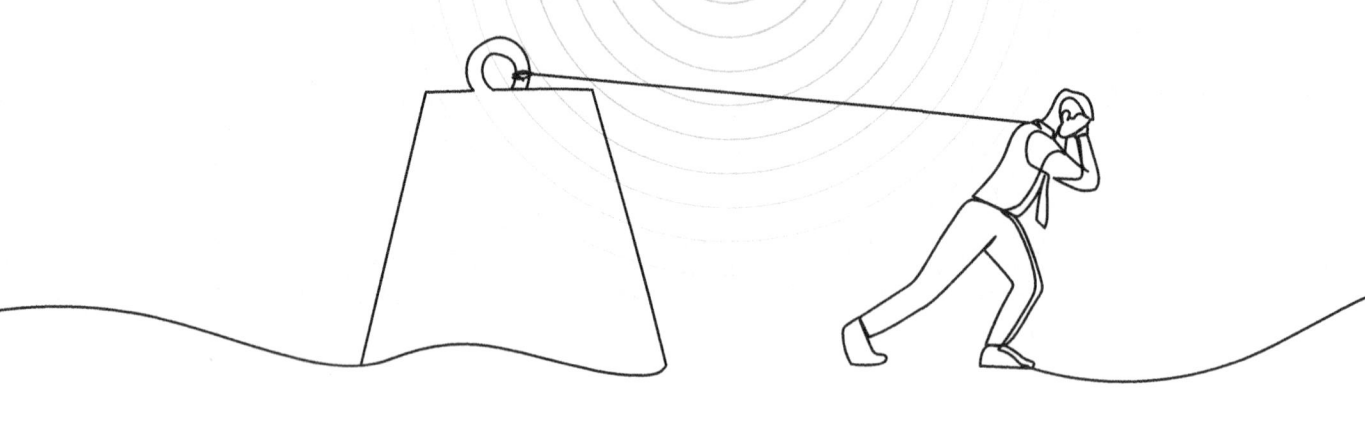

Experiencing the weight gain effects of a hormone imbalance becomes an unavoidable stage of life for both women and men when they enter menopause and andropause. Let's take an overview look first at the weight challenges faced by women during and after menopause when misfiring hormones (and loss of estrogen) are accelerating, even as body metabolisms are slowing down during advanced aging.

As a woman's estrogen levels decline in her 40's and 50's, her metabolic rate (how fast her metabolism burns calories) slows down. Then a double whammy occurs, like a series of falling dominoes being set in motion. In most women, less estrogen produces insomnia, which in turn increases the levels of the stress hormone cortisol, and that results in still more fat storage around the waist. With less estrogen, a biological urge emerges to engage in more sedentary and energy-saving behaviors, producing…you guessed it…greater weight gain from lack of exercise!

After a woman leaves menopause, lower estrogen levels often cause fat storage in cells to move from the thighs and hips to the abdomen, creating the 'post-meno belly' that many women fear, not just because of how it looks, but because this visceral fat increases their risk for heart disease, high blood pressure, and diabetes. By following a group of women pre-menopause through to post-menopause, University of Vermont School of Medicine scientists were able to persuasively document these changes in body fat distribution. They discovered that post-menopause, the women test subjects had 36% more trunk fat on average, 49% greater intra-abdominal fat, and 22% greater subcutaneous abdominal fat than at pre-menopause.

As we relate in Part Three, while these statistics may make it sound like most menopausal and postmenopausal women face a hopeless future in keeping the weight off, there are science-proven antidotes providing opportunities for winning the battle of the bulge.

For men, this hormone decline (particularly in testosterone) and resultant weight gain ignited by the aging process has been well-documented in the science literature for a decade, but the term describing it - Andropause - remains virtually unknown by most men and even disavowed by some physicians.

Scientists from Belgium and the United Kingdom provided a huge piece of the male midlife weight gain puzzle in 2015 when they published their test monitoring results involving 3,369 European men aged 40 to 79 years of age. Those men with the lowest testosterone levels were uniformly found to be at the highest risk for developing metabolic disorders characterized by large weight gains in their mid-sections.

(For more information on this male life stage, read our book, *Mano-Pause.*)

With our advancing years often comes still another challenge to our weight maintenance efforts----sleep disruption.

Toth MJ. Et al. "Menopause-related changes in body fat distribution." Ann NY Acad Sci. 2000 May.
Antonio L. Et al. "Associations between sex steroids and the development of metabolic syndrome: a longitudinal study in European men." J Clin Endocrinol Metab. 2015 April.

Short *and* Long Sleep Duration Promotes Obesity

If you habitually sleep on average five hours or less a night, or you sleep more than eight hours a night, both lifestyle habits have been found to encourage your body to store fat, especially if you are middle-aged and beyond.

A group of 19,709 adult volunteers aged 45 to 75 years, was studied by scientists at Uppsala University in Sweden, who assessed the volunteer's sleep habits and body composition. An analysis was also done of their leisure time, physical activities, and smoking and alcohol consumption.

In the study findings, published in a 2019 edition of the *Journal of Clinical Sleep Medicine*, these scientists reported a clear pattern showing that six to seven hours a night of quality sleep helped to protect against gaining weight. Any habitual number of hours under or over that duration resulted in a propensity to produce a higher fat body composition. The causative reasons for this phenomenon didn't seem apparent and more investigation was called for.

Previous research with children had found similar enlargement impacts on weight for *short-duration sleep*. British scientists from the University of Southampton, in 2016, took 302 boys and 285 girls and examined the association between their sleep habits at three years of age compared to their body composition and fat gain at four years of age. Their TV watching, dietary quality, and hours spent engaged in vigorous activity were also taken into account. What emerged from the observational data was a pattern persuasively demonstrating that shorter sleep hours produced a higher body mass index and more fat mass between the ages of three and four years.

Tan X. Et al. "Association Between Self-Reported Sleep Duration and Body Composition in Middle-aged and Older Adults." J Clin Sleep Med. 2019 March.
Baird J. Et al. "Duration of sleep at 3 years of age is associated with fat and fat-free mass at 4 years of age: the Southampton Women's Survey." J Sleep Res. 2016 August.

To provide an explanation for the causes of this association between poor sleep and weight gain, University of Chicago School of Medicine scientists pored over the study literature and concluded: "Sleep is an important modulator of neuroendocrine function and glucose metabolism and sleep loss has been shown to result in metabolic and endocrine alterations, including decreased glucose tolerance, decreased insulin sensitivity, increased evening concentrations of cortisol, increased levels of ghrelin (the hormone that controls energy storage as fat), decreased levels of leptin (the hormone that regulates appetite and metabolism), and increased hunger and appetite."

As an illustration of how powerful chronic impaired sleep's impact on fat retention can be, medical researchers at the Cedars-Sinai Medical Center in Los Angeles tested sleep deprivation and a high-fat diet on animals and discovered that *one night of poor sleep can equal six months on a high-fat diet*. These study results, presented to The Obesity Society annual conference in 2015, seemed to show a similar mechanism by which a high-fat diet and poor sleep induce insulin resistance, both of which have a negative result of producing weight gain and a higher risk for diabetes.

Research focusing on the direct impact that chronic inadequate sleep has on the brain shows a decreased activity in the parts of the frontal cortex that govern evaluation and regulation of food desire, combined with an amplification of activity within those brain parts likely responsible for "selecting high-calorie foods most capable of triggering weight gain," said the 2013 report in the science journal, Nature Communications. It's no wonder that many people feel totally out of control in the face of food cravings which their brains seem incapable of regulating because the appetite-promoting hormones leptin and ghrelin have gone haywire.

There seems to be a biological evolutionary reason why our bodies react to poor sleep by storing fat. "Our findings suggest that increased food intake during insufficient sleep is a physiological adaptation to provide energy needed to sustain additional wakefulness, yet when food is easily accessible, intake surpasses what is needed," wrote scientists in a 2013 issue of the *Proceedings of the National Academy of Sciences USA*.

One cause of chronic sleep disruption and resulting weight gain, a factor too few people recognize or sufficiently appreciate, is caused by exposure to any level of light source when attempting to sleep at night. In a study of 100,000 women aged 16 years and older in Britain, scientists found "a significant association between LAN (light at night) exposure and obesity," they wrote, which affirmed results from animal experiments. Unless you sleep in total darkness, ambient

---

Beccuti G. Pannain S. "Sleep and obesity." Curr Opin Clin Nutr Metab Care. 2013 April.
Broussard J. Et al. "One night of poor sleep could equal six months on a high-fat diet, study in dogs suggests." ScienceDaily. November 4, 2015. Greer SM. Et al. "The impact of sleep deprivation on food desire in the human brain." Nature Communications. 2013 February.

light exposure in the room where you sleep "can increase the risk of obesity and the metabolic syndrome by disrupting circadian and circannual rhythms."

The human body's circadian biological clock regulates energy balance, cellular and physiological processes, and this system is synchronized by light information. Numerous studies have shown how "low levels of light at night disrupt the timing of food intake and other metabolic signals, leading to excess weight gain," reported a 2010 study from Ohio State University.

Other studies similarly document how diets high in fat or sugar also play a role in altering circadian clock functions, which, when added to the impacts of sleep deprivation from ambient light, further magnifies the negative effects that occur on feeding behaviors and the body's fat storage mechanisms.

Last but not by any means least, let's not forget what generally disrupts sleep more than any other factor - chronic stress.

Markwald RR. Et al. "Impact of insufficient sleep on total daily energy expenditure, food intake, and weight gain." Proc Natl Acad Sci USA. 2013 April.
McFadden E. Et al. "The relationship between obesity and exposure to light at night: cross-sectional analyses of over 100,000 women in the Breakthrough Generations Study." Am J Epidemiol. 2014 August. Also, Gangwisch JE. "Invited commentary: nighttime light exposure as a risk factor for obesity through disruption of circadian and circannual rhythms." Am J Epidemiol. 2014 August.
Fonken LK. Et al. "Light at night increases body mass by shifting the time of food intake." Proc Natl Acad Sci USA. 2010 October. Oosterman JE. Et al. "Impact of nutrients on circadian rhythmicity." Am J Physiol Regul Integr Comp Physiol. 2015 March.

Chronic Stress Influences Your Weight

Anyone at any stage of their life can be impacted by chronic stress, most particularly while under job or financial pressure or when enduring traumatic events such as deaths, births, or divorces. In short, daily life itself equals stress. The key weight influencer is the stress hormone cortisol, secreted by the adrenal gland.

While it's true that some people react to chronic psychological stress by starving themselves and, thus, losing weight in the short term, most people react with emotional eating, which alters their metabolism to encourage weight gain. A Yale University School of Medicine review of the scientific findings on stress and weight found, in 2018, how "stress hormones hijack the brain's emotional (limbic) and motivational (striatal) pathways, to promote food craving and excessive food intake." High levels of stress were also seen to alter the body's metabolism, producing higher weight and altered insulin sensitivity.

Because our evolutionary history primed our bodies to react to threats by producing instant bursts of energy via cortisol, our bodies were also designed to store abdominal fat in response as a sort of energy insurance policy for future survival. That worked well for our species in the ancient past, but today it's an outdated software program that warps our metabolism with disordered eating patterns. We are quite literally storing fat we no longer need for individual or species survival.

When chronic stress arises from feelings of anxiety and loneliness, as affects many people, weight gain may be one repercussion. Putting on pounds can also result from prolonged periods of financial distress, and this is an area which has been rigorously studied by scientists.

If you grew up in, or continue to live in, a socioeconomically disadvantaged area, you are automatically exposed to high levels of stress that increases your chances for obesity. This phenomenon was documented in a 2016 science study in the journal, *Stress*, in which a large group of women and children from economically depressed neighborhoods had cortisol levels in their hair measured and compared to their weight, body mass index (BMI), and their results from taking a Perceived Stress Scale test. Their stress scores "were positively associated with their BMI," the research team concluded.

Sinha R. "Role of addiction and stress neurobiology on food intake and obesity." Biol Psychol. 2018 January.

One bit of irony surrounding stress and weight is that obese and overweight men (much more than women) secrete high levels of stress hormones *after* each meal they eat, further increasing their risk for weight gain, as well as making them more susceptible to a range of stress-related diseases. This finding came from testing 17 overweight or obese men and comparing them to normal-weight men of a similar age, between 50 and 70 years. Saliva samples were taken from the study participants after meals to measure their cortisol concentrations. Among the overweight and obese men, cortisol levels rose by 51%, compared to only five percent among the normal weight men.

This finding prompted the lead study author, Anne Turner, Ph.D., to observe: "This research indicates that when we are carrying excess fat stores, we may also be exposing our bodies to increased levels of the stress hormone cortisol every time we have a meal." She said this places men at greater risk for stress-related diseases, such as cardiovascular disease, along with attracting additional weight gain.

The science-proven antidote to chronic stress can be found in the pages of this book. It involves meditation, mindfulness, and relaxation techniques that are portable, easy to use, and easy to learn.

Your Cell Phone May Play a Role

Research is underway on the stress and weight impact of human exposure to electromagnetic fields, particularly those emitted by cell phones and other gadgets. Based on preliminary findings, however, we need to include this technology in assessing the stress and weight gain linkages. "EMPs impact melatonin and sleep, which results in more carb cravings and cortisol surges," observed Louise Gittleman, Ph.D., author of *Zapped: Why Your Cell Phone Shouldn't Be Your Alarm Clock and 1,268 Ways to Outsmart the Hazards of Electronic Pollution.*

Partial support for Gittleman's findings came from a 2011 study in the *Journal of the American Medical Association,* in which scientists monitored the brain effects of a 50-minute cell phone conversation among 47 healthy adults. Brain glucose metabolism levels were measured in each study participant before and after cell phone use. Compared to test subjects who had no cell phone exposure, those on the 50-minute calls showed "increased brain glucose metabolism in the {brain} region closest to the {phone} antenna." While the implications are still being studied, these findings seem to suggest radiofrequency signals can interrupt brain mechanisms related to body metabolism control, fitting the pattern seen in other research on the connection between warped metabolism signaling and resultant weight gain.

Volkow ND. Et al. "Effects of cell phone radiofrequency signal exposure on brain glucose metabolism." JAMA. 2011 February.

More recent scientific findings provide new disturbing evidence for a link between cell phone usage and weight gain. German scientists in 2022, exposed 15 normal-weight young men, average age 23 years, to 25 minutes of radio frequency-modulated electromagnetic fields emitted by two different mobile phone types. In the aftermath, their food intake was monitored. According to the findings, published in the science journal Nutrients, "exposure to both mobile phones strikingly increased overall caloric intake by 22-27% …and higher calorie consumption was mainly due to enhanced carbohydrate intake."

All of these results, taken together, strongly indicate that mobile phone electromagnetic field emissions are a contributing factor to the overeating which fuels the obesity epidemic. Along with limiting your cell phone usage in general, you might want to consider stopping all phone usage altogether before and during your meals.

Wardzinski EK. Et al. "Mobile Phone Radiation Deflects Brain Energy Homeostasis and Prompts Human Food Ingestion." Nutrients. 2022 January.

Insulin Resistance Triggers Weight Gain

Results from multiple science studies demonstrate that adult weight gain is strongly associated with increased insulin resistance. In turn, weight gain and obesity are causal risk factors for type 2 diabetes, cardiovascular disease, and certain cancers.

"Insulin is a metabolic hormone made by the pancreas when you eat, that tells your body's cells that fuel, in the form of blood sugar or glucose, is available for immediate use," according to the Scripps Clinic Center for Weight Management. "In some cases, the body's cells don't respond to insulin as they should and can't easily take sugar from the blood. The pancreas reacts by producing more insulin to try to keep up with higher blood sugar levels."

Excess abdominal fat around the waist (the so-called 'beer belly') combined with insufficient physical activity, rank as the biggest triggers for insulin resistance, along with a diet of highly processed carbohydrate foods and saturated fats. Collect fat around your midsection and your body is primed to accumulate more fat there. Symptoms of insulin resistance you should watch for include the slow healing of cuts and sores, headaches, blurred vision, increased hunger, frequent urination, and increased thirst. "Can Insulin Resistance Cause Weight Gain?"

Canadian naturopathic doctor and hormone expert, Lara Briden, says insulin resistance is more common than most of us suspect, and this condition could be affecting you, even if your blood sugar measurements seem to be in the 'normal' range. She defines insulin resistance as a "dysfunction of the metabolic nuts and bolts of the cell that are supposed to turn food into energy. The result of that

---

"The Association between Adult Weight Gain and Insulin Resistance at Middle Age: Meditation by Visceral Fat and Liver Fat." Verkouter I. Et al. Journal of Clinical Medicine. 2019 October.
Scripps Organization News. June 7, 2022. https://www.scripps.org/news_items/4621-can-insulin-resistance-cause-weight-gain

metabolic dysfunction is less energy, more inflammation, high cholesterol, high triglycerides and importantly, something called fatty liver, which is fat accumulation in the liver. Actually, fatty liver is both caused by insulin resistance and a cause of insulin resistance."

High insulin levels drive weight gain and also indicate underlying metabolic dysfunctions. Dr. Briden identifies the signs of insulin resistance as fatty liver and weight gain around the waist, but also the presence of skin tags and the darkening of the skin around the armpits and neck. She recommends taking a simple fasting insulin test, or a glucose tolerance test with insulin, to determine if you have insulin resistance. (See Part Three for how you can reverse insulin resistance.)

Mix Stress with Toxins; You Get Fatter

We can now add early-life exposure to certain toxic chemicals, which disrupt the body's endocrine system (the network of glands that secrete hormones to control metabolism), to the list of 'traditional risk factors' for obesity. These toxins are called obesogens and get magnified by stress to interact in the body, confuse your hormones, and attract additional excess pounds.

In a review of the scientific evidence for obesogens, a team of researchers identified, in 2018, numerous categories of toxins we come in contact with that will fatten us. They act by confusing our hormones and metabolism to trigger both childhood obesity and further weight gain later in life. These chemicals appear in pesticides, herbicides, plastics, detergents, flame retardants, metal food cans, industrial and household products, as well as intentionally added ingredients in a variety of personal care products commonly sold.

How this process occurs in the human body to produce weight gain has been studied and debated by toxicologists over the past decade. According to the science journal, *Archives of Toxicology*, in 2017: "The mechanisms of action of obesogens lay on their ability to increase the number and/or the size of adipocytes {which store calories and maintain energy balance} and to alter appetite, satiety and food preferences. The ability of obesogens to increase fat deposition results in an increased capacity for their own retention due to their lipophilic {ability to dissolve in fat} properties, thus prolonging the exposure and increasing the detrimental metabolic consequences."

Yang C. Et al. "Early-life exposure to endocrine disrupting chemicals associates with childhood obesity." Ann Pediatr Endocrinol Metab. 2018 December.
Muscogiuri G. Et al. "Obesogenic endocrine disruptors and obesity: myths and truths." Arch Toxicol. 2017 November.

To further underscore what we have just described, the ability of obesogens to increase fat deposits in the body "has the added consequence of increasing the capacity for their own retention," emphasizes P.D. Darbre, a professor of biological sciences at Britain's University of Reading. "This has the potential for a vicious spiral not only of increasing obesity but also increasing the retention of other lipophilic pollutant chemicals with an even broader range of adverse actions. This might offer an explanation as to why obesity is an underlying risk factor for so many diseases, including cancer."

You're starting to get a picture of why these toxins are such a hidden danger to human weight and health. They are conniving and clever, and they are lurking everywhere around us. When absorbed by the body, they behave like estrogen, and this fake estrogen overwhelms the body's stores of testosterone, setting in motion serious hormone imbalances. This may be why so many young girls enter puberty earlier than ever before, and why some boys are showing breast growth.

We know that depending on the mother's diet, fat accumulations for babies later in life can be predisposed in the womb. Exposure to these environmental obesogens may also predispose babies and even fetuses in the womb, via the mother's exposure, "to increased fat mass and excess weight," according to scientific studies reviewed in the *Journal of Environmental & Public Health*. This predisposition to fat storage can show up in both childhood and at various stages of adulthood.

"There is an urgent, unmet need to understand the mechanisms underlying how exposure to certain EDCs {endocrine disrupting compounds} may predispose our population to be obese," warned the authors of a 2016 study, which appeared in the *American Journal of Obstetrics and Gynecology*.

Some of these mechanisms are becoming clearer with each passing year. Obesogens act on the estrogen, androgen, and thyroid hormone receptors, to disrupt the human hormone metabolism, causing weight gain. These toxins alter the programming of fat cells and interfere with appetite control.

The list of synthetic chemicals having obesogen effects continues to multiply, as do the mechanisms linked to obesity. In a 2020 issue of the science journal, *Endocrinology,* for instance, links were drawn between BPA exposure (bisphenol A is found in plastic containers that store food and beverages) and changes in the gut microbiome composition, which help to manage metabolism. Such an effect on a child in the womb, through the mother's exposure, could predispose the child to develop a gut microbiome that accelerates weight gain.

Darbre PD. "Endocrine Disruptors and Obesity." Curr Obes Rep. 2017 March.
Kelishadi R. Et al. "Role of Environmental Chemicals in Obesity: A Systematic Review on the Current Evidence." J Environ Public Health. 2013. Janesick AS. Blumberg B. "Obesogens: an emerging threat to public health." Am J Obstet & Gynecology. 2016.

You may wonder, as we do, how many well-known, seemingly well-intentioned dietitians and weight loss program consultants bother to inform their clients of these obesogens as contributing factors to obesity. These conversations should be normalized to facilitate the implementation of treatment plans that work in the long term for weight loss.

Riann JE. Blumberg B. "Environmental Obesogens and Their Impact on Susceptibility to Obesity: New Mechanism and Chemicals." Endocrinology. 2020 March.

Beware of These Serious Chemical Offenders

How many types of hormone-disrupting obesogens, on average, populate your body fat? According to a report by the Environmental Working group, which reviewed blood testing samples of volunteers at the Mount Sinai School of Medicine in New York, you probably shelter at least 58 types of hormone-disruptive chemicals - and that's a conservative estimate. These constitute what toxicologists call your "body burden" of absorption.

Here are some of the more common chemical invaders which may be contributing to your weight gain and your long-term inability to shed those pounds.

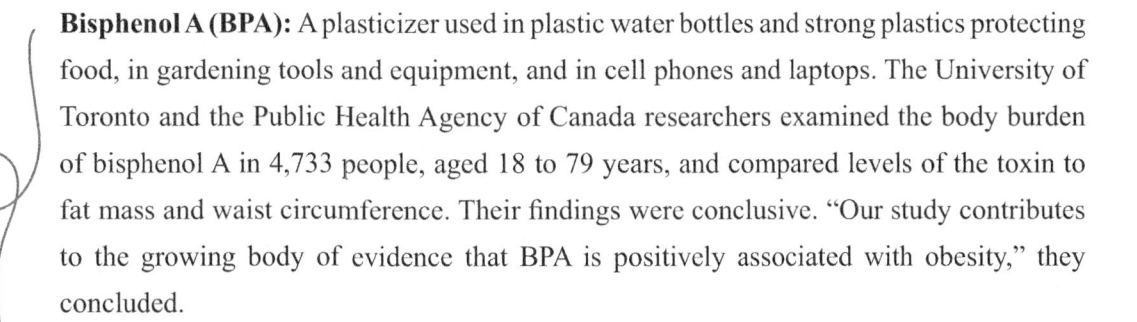

Bisphenol A (BPA): A plasticizer used in plastic water bottles and strong plastics protecting food, in gardening tools and equipment, and in cell phones and laptops. The University of Toronto and the Public Health Agency of Canada researchers examined the body burden of bisphenol A in 4,733 people, aged 18 to 79 years, and compared levels of the toxin to fat mass and waist circumference. Their findings were conclusive. "Our study contributes to the growing body of evidence that BPA is positively associated with obesity," they concluded.

Nonylphenol: Used in manufacturing laundry and dish detergents, in many different personal care products, and a variety of plastics. A 2012 study assessing the impact Nonylphenol has on fat cells reached this conclusion: "it may be expected to increase the incidence of obesity and can act as a potential chemical stressor for obesity and obesity-related disorders."

Environmental Working Group. "BodyBurden: Findings & Recommendations." www.ewg.org/sites/bodyburden1/findings.php
Do MT. Et al. "Urinary bisphenol A and obesity in adults: results from the Canadian Health Measures Survey." Health Promot Chornic Dis Prev Can. 2017 December.
Hao CJ. Et al. "The endocrine disrupter 4-nonylphenol promotes adipocyte differentiation and induces obesity in mice." Cell Physiol Biochem. 2012.

Perfluorinated Compounds (PFCs): Used in industrial products and processes to make coatings that resist heat, oil, stains, grease, and water. They are used in the production of Teflon-casted kitchenware.

Scientists in Denmark, at the University of Southern Denmark, did a 2016 study in which they examined more than 1,000 children, taking blood samples at various year stages of their lives to detect levels of the perfluorinated chemicals PFOS and PFOA. Their conclusion: "Childhood exposure was associated with indicators of {obesity} at 15 years of age that are displayed in elevated BMI, skinfold thickness, and waist circumference, as well as increased skinfold thickness and waist circumference at 21 years of age."

Persistent Organic Pollutants (POPs): These include PCBs, DDE, dioxin, and related pesticides, which are resistant to breaking down over time in the environment, making them 'persistent' in their toxic effects. Their link with obesity in humans has been thoroughly studied.

For example, in a 2013 issue of the science journal, Obesity, a study described how 1,016 test subjects, average age of 70 years, were investigated. Blood testing revealed the presence of 23 different POPs. Using measures of waist circumference and fat mass as obesity markers, it was found that the higher the levels of POPs in the bodies of test subjects, the more likely they were to be obese.

A 2014 study in the Journal of Clinical Endocrinology & Metabolism, blood tested 76 obese, postmenopausal women. Those with the lowest levels of 21 POPs had more normal body mass indexes, whereas the women showing the higher levels of POPs were more obese. This was particularly true the higher their body levels of dioxin.

Phthalates: These fragrance carrier chemicals are found in personal care products, shower curtains, and a range of other products, including building materials, such as PVC pipe. Studies show that phthalates impair the human body's regulation of fat metabolism and impair testosterone production.

Domazet SL. Et al. "Longitudinal Associations of Exposure to Perfluoroalkylated Substances in Childhood and Adolescence and Indicators of Adiposity and Glucose Metabolism 6 and 12 Years Later: The European Youth Heart Study." Diabetes Care. 2016 October.
Roos V. Et al. "Circulation levels of persistent organic pollutants in relation to visceral and subcutaneous adipose tissue by abdominal MRI." Obesity. 2013 February.
Gauthier MS. Et al. "The metabolically healthy but obese phenotype is associated with lower plasma levels of persistent organic pollutants as compared to the metabolically abnormal obese phenotype." J Clin Endocrinol Metab. 2014 June.

To illustrate the scientific study findings, a major endocrinology journal published a study in 2017 in which blood and urine samples were taken from 132 obese and 64 overweight persons aged 17 to 62 years. "Total blood/urinary phthalate levels significantly increased in proportion to the degree of obesity," the science team concluded, "showing a strong association between obesity and phthalates."

Tributyltin: An agricultural fungicide and antimicrobial compound used in plastics and industrial water systems. By reviewing 22 science studies on synthetic chemicals and their relationship to obesity, University of Michigan School of Public Health scientists identified tributyltin as a possible culprit in triggering weight gain and obesity, especially at early ages when exposure to this chemical first begins in life.

Triclosan: An antibacterial and antifungal agent found in everything from toothpaste, some soaps, shampoos, deodorants, bedding, socks, detergents and even some children's toys. In 2017, the U.S. Food and Drug Administration ordered the removal of triclosan from consumer antiseptic wash products because of its effects on hormonal development in children.

Stanford University School of Medicine scientists examined the relationship between triclosan and body mass index in 2013 by assessing nationwide results of urinary triclosan levels compiled from the National Health and Nutrition Examination Surveys. They found unmistakable evidence that "triclosan exposure is associated with increased body mass index."

It's so challenging to get rid of chemical toxins because once they enter the cell, they confuse the cells and change the rhythm and the way each cell interacts with other cells. Creating abnormal cells ends up creating abnormal tissue.

Chemical manufacturers would like us to believe that the body burden levels of obesogen molecules we carry around in our bodies from toxins we absorb are so tiny as to have no impact on our health and our weight. This assumption ignores two complicating factors - the cumulative impact of these chemical exposures absorbed over a lifetime, and the additive or synergistic impacts these chemicals have as they are interacting with each other inside our fat tissues.

Oktar S. Et al. "The relationship between phthalates and obesity: serum and urine concentrations of phthalates." Minerva Endocrinol. 2017 March.
Liu Y. Et al. "Maternal Exposure to Synthetic Chemicals and Obesity in the Offspring: Recent Findings." Curr Environ Health Rep. 2015 December. Lankester J. Et al. "Urinary Triclosan is Associated with Elevated Body Mass Index in NHANES." PLoS One. 2013.

Three Categories of Products Give Chemical Exposure

Our contact with these obesogen contaminants most often comes from three categories of products in daily use: our food products, personal care products, and our clothing.

Food Contamination: Our food supply, particularly meat, fish, and dairy products, have become a major route of exposure. One especially pesky group of contaminants are PBDEs, flame retardants used in mattresses and other products, which leach these chemicals into the surrounding air.

Scientists at the University of Texas Health Science Center surveyed 30 food types, testing samples off the shelves of major supermarket chain stores in Dallas, Texas. Flame retardants "were {found in} almost exclusively foods of animal origin: meat, fish, and dairy products," the researchers reported in the journal *Environmental Science & Technology*. The highest levels were found in fish. Furthermore, "PBDE levels measured in this study are higher than reported in two other published market-based studies from Spain and Japan."

Thirteen different types of PBDEs were examined in a 2008 review of studies that had measured PBDEs in both food and mother's milk samples. Results were similar to food findings in previous studies, but the big surprise came in measurements of the obesogen body burden in women, being passed on to their babies via milk ingestion. "All US women's breast milk samples were contaminated with PBDEs," the review found. The levels were in "orders of magnitude, higher than levels reported in European studies, and are the highest reported worldwide."

Schecter A. Et al. "Polybrominated diphenyl ethers contamination of United States food." Environ Sci Technol. 2004 October.

Personal Care Contamination: A wide array of cosmetics and personal care products have been infused with hormone-disrupting obesogens, such as phthalates found in some brands of lipsticks, and parabens added to some deodorants and antiperspirants as a preservative.

Many of these and other hormone-disruptor chemicals were identified in a 2009 book, Toxic Beauty, by University of Illinois toxicologist, Dr. Samuel S. Epstein. He detailed at least 30, appearing in cosmetics and personal care products, grouped under the categories of preservatives - such as triclosan and parabens - and detergents, solvents, metalloestrogens, lavender and tea tree oil, and sunscreens. This latter category of sunscreens presents particularly dangerous challenges because the six obesogen chemicals commonly used in them are slathered over much of the skin and absorbed quickly into the bloodstream.

Two reliable resources for identifying obesogens and other toxins in cosmetics and personal care products, as well as revealing companies that manufacture safe products, are: The Campaign for Safe Cosmetics (www.safecosmetics.org) and The Environmental Working Group's Skin Deep Database (www.cosmeticsdatabase.com)

Clothing Contamination: It may come as a surprise to learn that most individual pieces of clothing sold in the industrialized world are manufactured to contain hundreds of different chemicals, quite a few of them with the potential to disrupt your hormone system and contribute to weight gain.

A disturbing report came from the Center for Environmental Health in the U.S., during 2022, which analyzed nearly a dozen common sports bra and athletic shirt brands and found high levels - up to 22 times the safe limit - of the chemical BPA, a well-known obesity enhancer, embedded in the spandex portion of the fabrics. When the wearer exercises and perspires, this chemical gets released onto the skin and absorbed into the bloodstream. BPA mimics hormones like estrogen and can disrupt the metabolism of both men and women. Who would have imagined that the act of perspiring during exercise could end up accelerating weight gain. "New Testing Shows High Levels of BPA in Sports Bras and Athletic Shirts."

Other treacherous hormone-disrupting obesity-enhancing chemicals embedded in clothing range from phthalates, fire retardants, and perfluorinated compounds, to heavy metals like

Schecter A. Et al. "Brominated flame retardants in US food." Mol Nutr Food Res. 2008 February.
Epstein, Samuel S., Fitzgerald, Randall. Toxic Beauty: Your Guide to Ingredients to Avoid and Products You Can Trust. 2009. BenBella Books: Dallas.

lead and cadmium. As we pointed out in our 2011 book, *Killer Clothes: How Seemingly Innocent Clothing Choices Endanger Your Health…And How to Protect Yourself!* the more synthetic clothing you own and wear, the greater your risk of absorbing toxic chemicals through your skin and into your bloodstream.

Let's give you one example of such a hidden danger. Permethrin is an insecticide applied to outdoor clothing fabrics, during the manufacturing process, as a repellent to help kill ticks, mosquitos, and other insects. This toxin-laden clothing is sold to people of all ages. As our book states, "a portion of all permethrin on clothing comes off on the skin and is absorbed by the skin," and given the findings of scientific studies, this means "people of every age who have worn these garments are guinea pigs in a long-term, uncontrolled experiment."

Permethrin is a documented hormone disruptor. Scientists in 2011, in lab animal experiments, discovered that permethrin had negative effects on body weight as a result of "hormonal disruption evidenced by the measurement of the plasma testosterone concentrations." The "significant disharmony in testosterone concentration," concluded the science team, was an effect related to dose and length of exposure to the chemical. Given that clothing treated with permethrin might be worn dozens if not hundreds of times, both the exposure time and dosages being absorbed should be cause for concern for anyone trying to control their weight.

> How can you get rid of contaminants already lodged in your fat tissue and lessen your body burden to help keep the weight off? Take a look at Part Three of this book, where we explain proven strategies for detoxifying your body.

Center for Environmental Health. October 12, 2022. https://ceh.org/latest/press-releases/new-testing-shows-high-levels-of-bpa-in-sports-bras-and-athletic-shirts/
Issam C. Et al. "Effects of dermal sub-chronic exposure of pubescent male rats to permethrin (PRMT) on the histological structures of genital tract, testosterone and lipoperoxidation." Exp Toxicol Pathol. 2011 May.

Don't Overlook the Impact of Your Medications

Obesogenic (weight-causing) prescription drugs are another hidden source of weight gain for some people that are too often overlooked when they start a weight loss diet or when health professionals assess a patient's overall health prior to entering a weight reduction program.

In a 2019 study of 666 adult patients at a Veterans Health Administration facility, it was found that 62% of them entering a behavioral weight loss program had prescriptions for obesogenic medications. That made them much less likely to achieve meaningful weight loss. "Patients who received three or more medications had the greatest difficulty achieving 5% weight loss," concluded the study research team, writing in the journal, *Obesity*.

To determine which classes of prescription drugs most often trigger weight gain, Mayo Clinic medical researchers did a systematic review of studies, 257 randomized clinical trials altogether, searching for evidence of weight gain as a side effect of drug testing. The studies involved more than 84,000 test subjects, ranging in age from 22 to 88 years.

The class of drugs with the biggest associated weight gain were atypical antipsychotics, including these drugs: olanzapine, quetiapine, and risperidone.

Second on the weight gain list were anticonvulsants and mood stabilizers, including these drugs: gabapentin and divalproex.

Desalermos A. Et al. "Effect of Obesogenic Medications on Weight-Loss Outcomes in a Behavioral Weight-Management Program." Obesity. 2019 May.

Next were drugs falling into the category of hypoglycemic agents, including tolbutamide, pioglitazone, glimepiride, gliclazide, glyburide, glipizide, sitagliptin, and nateglinide.

Hormone-related drugs with weight gain side effects include glucocorticoids used in rheumatoid arthritis.

Antidepressants such as amitriptyline and mirtazapine were associated with weight gain.

Needless to say, if you are taking any of the above medications, and determine they are partially responsible for your weight gain or your inability to maintain a healthy weight, it might be worthwhile to consult with your healthcare specialist about alternative medications that would be safe and effective for you to use instead of the obesogenic drugs.

Finally, don't overlook steroids and the role they can play in weight gain. A case in point is Prednisone, taken primarily for arthritic conditions. "Weight gain is a common side effect of prednisone," declared the University of California at San Francisco website, based on the consensus of study findings.

You would be well served by making a list of all your daily medications and comparing them to the weight promoter listing in the preceding paragraphs. You might also do Google searches under terms such as 'prescription drug weight promoters' and 'drugs that cause weight gain' to identify any others that may be contributing to your weight challenges. Then confer with your physician or pharmacist about alternatives that are more weight- friendly.

Domecq JP. Et al. "Drugs Commonly Associated With Weight Change: A Systematic Review and Meta-Analysis." J Clin Endocrinol Metab. 2015 February.
"Prednisone and Weight Gain." UCSF Health. www.ucsfhealth.org/education/ild-nutrition-manual-prednisone-and-weight-gain

Hidden Triggers for Food Cravings

Craving foods that help to fatten us up - the so-called 'comfort' foods - means we feel a psychological compulsion triggered by two stimulators: food-specific cues, such as colors, smells, and even sounds we unconsciously associate with a food we crave, and environmental cues, such as social gatherings and settings, which program food consumption habits we find hard to break.

Most of us are subjected to an almost constant daily barrage of these food-specific and environmental cues. Whether it's a craving prompted by the sound of a potato chip bag opening nearby or a memory awakened of a previous snack food binge at a party, it's a response registered in an area of our brain dedicated to sensing pleasure. In that regard, cravings truly are 'all in our head.'

This helps to explain why trying to change our behaviors to consume only healthy foods, or to eat less and exercise more, can be such a persistent challenge. University of Vermont psychologist Mark Bouton, who has co-authored dozens of scientific studies on this subject, points out "that changing a behavior can be an inherently unstable and unsteady process; frequent lapses should be expected." This observation comes from research suggesting that most methods used to initiate behavior change - counterconditioning, abstinence, punishment, etc. - tend to inhibit rather than erase the unhealthy behavior. Unless the underlying context within which the behavior was learned is directly addressed - for example, childhood abuse that prompted overeating - then our relapses become almost inevitable.

Bouton ME. "Why behavior change is difficult to sustain." Prev Med. 2014 November.

While these observations are quite important in our understanding of food cravings and how to control, if not banish them, we also need to be aware of the broader societal context within which we function and the attendant manipulators at work to influence our food behaviors and ultimately, create our unwanted excess weight. Specifically, we are talking about food product manufacturers who seek to intentionally exploit our psychological weaknesses for their financial gain.

We know that food cravings often arise simply to satisfy our emotional needs, as when we need to reduce anxiety or to calm stress. Here we are back to the role that 'comfort' foods play, particularly when these foods are created by food chemists to change our brain chemistry and cause us to crave even more. A good illustration comes in the form of potato chips.

Harvard Medical School researchers examined medical data on 120,877 U.S. women and men over a 20-year period. Within each 4-year period, these study participants gained an average of 3.3 pounds. This weight gain "was most strongly associated with the intake of potato chips, potatoes, sugar-sweetened beverages, and processed meats," the science team concluded.

In an attempt to understand why it's easier for many people to eat an entire bag of potato chips rather than just one (you know that old advertising slogan, bet you can't eat just one!), scientists published a 2011 study in the *Proceedings of the National Academy of Sciences*, that described a neural mechanism underlying the brain's preference for fatty foods like potato chips. Once consumed, potato chips stimulate the human body to produce chemicals that resemble the cannabinoids in marijuana. These endocannabinoids, as they are referred to, get produced and secreted from the gut and send out signals "exerting a powerful regulatory control over fat intake," reported the science team.

Potato chips contain an almost equal combination of calories from fat and calories from carbohydrates. Food chemists working within the food processing industry know how to manipulate these combinations to achieve the most potent 'brain rewards', leading to addictive behaviors when these highly processed foods are consumed in snack food products. (See more later in this section of the book on how this usually works.)

Something else to keep in mind about cravings is that scientific research indicates that we often crave what we last ate. Yale University School of Medicine scientists did a clinical trial with 91 overweight and obese persons, average age of 43 years, to see what food cravings were correlated with the consumption of corresponding types of foods. The results indicated that the cravings for

---

Mozaffarian D. Et al. "Changes in diet and lifestyle and long term weight gain in women and men." N Engl J Med. 2011 June. DiPatrizio NV. Et al. "Endocannabinoid signal in the gut controls dietary fat intake." Proc Natl Acad Sci USA. 2011 August.

high-fat savory snacks like potato chips were connected to a time frame within which potato chips were earlier repetitively consumed. In other words, the type of conditioning involved for this food preference to repetitively emerge resembles nothing less than an addiction.

Let's take a deeper dive into exactly how hidden triggers for food cravings and subsequent weight gain combine to manipulate us as a result of the food industry's intricately laid plans using consumers as an ongoing deviously clever chemistry experiment.

Martin CK. Et al. "The association between food cravings and consumption of specific foods in a laboratory taste test." Appetite. 2008 September.

Food Advertising Makes You Eat More

While we all like to think we are in control of our thoughts, actions, and our lives, when it comes to our food preferences and our food compulsions, we are constantly influenced to over-indulge by the not-so-hidden persuaders of food cues buried in various forms of advertising. Our contention is backed by a series of psychological studies done on the effects of food advertisements on eating behaviors among both children and adults.

In two experiments 160 female undergraduate students and 124 overweight non-student women, were exposed to food advertising and then took a battery of tests assessing the impact on their

Kemps E. Et al. "Exposure to television food advertising primes food-related cognitions and triggers motivation to eat." Psychology & Health. 2014.

cognitive processes, motivations to eat, and the extent they were able to exercise control over their compulsions. As reported in the journal, *Psychology & Health,* the food advertising activated brain functions related to desire in most of the women, but most particularly a stronger desire to eat among women who were already overweight.

These results shouldn't be considered surprising since, as the study authors observed, "approximately a third to half of all television advertisements are for food. Of these, the majority are for unhealthy food that is high in fat, sugar, and/or salt with little nutritional value. Recent studies show that exposure to television advertisements promoting snack foods increases snack food intake in both adults and children. Food advertising stimulates people's desire to eat and motivation to act."

Other studies have even calculated how much more unhealthy food young people consume after exposure to food advertising. Scientists writing in the journal, *Health Psychology*, did experiments with elementary-school-age children who watched a cartoon that contained food advertising, or advertising for other products during which they received a snack while watching. "Children consumed 45% more when exposed to food advertising," the study concluded. "These experiments demonstrate the power of food advertising to prime automatic eating behaviors and thus influence far more than brand preference alone."

So, the difficulty that chronic dieters experience in pursuing their weight loss goals can be at least partially explained by their being surrounded by "palatable food cues that strongly prime the goal of eating enjoyment and facilitate unhealthy eating," as the science journal, *Psychological Review* observed.

There is, however, a bright spot in this body of research findings that offers hope to everyone who has tried and failed to summon willpower. As *Psychological Review* noted: "There is a minority of restrained eaters for whom, most likely due to past success in exerting self-control, tasty high-calorie food has become associated with weight control thoughts. For them, exposure to palatable food increases the accessibility of the weight control goal, enabling them to control their body weight in food-rich environments."

One advertising theme we must never overlook is the so-called 'diet' products marketed with weight loss claims, which are tricking consumers.

Harris JL. Et al. "Priming effects of television food advertising on eating behavior." Health Psychol. 2009 July.
Stroebe W. Et al. "Why most dieters fail but some succeed: a goal conflict model of eating behavior." Psychol Rev. 2013 January.

Diet Products Can Cause Weight Gain

People who use diet drinks and related 'dietary' products containing artificial sweeteners, thinking this will help them lose weight, have lulled themselves into a false sense of health security.

Rather than being non-fattening and healthier than non-dietary products, diet soda and similar 'foods' containing artificial sweeteners confuse the human metabolism, resulting in weight gain. This is the remarkable conclusion of scientific studies examining how and why these artificial sweeteners confuse the brain and body about their true caloric value, which ends up contributing to obesity and metabolic disorders.

Some of the most pioneering research showing this linkage appeared in 2017, when neuroscientists at Yale University assembled a group of human volunteers and had them drink five different beverages containing varying levels of sweetener calories. All five of the drinks were sweetened with the artificial sweetener, sucralose, and all five tasted equally sweet, but they contained this range of calories---zero, 37.5, 75, 112.5, and 150. (Calories had been diluted and masked using the addition of maltodextrin, a tasteless carbohydrate.)

What emerged from weeks of testing, in which the volunteers had fMRI brain scans after consuming each drink to measure their body's metabolic response, surprised the investigators. The 75-calorie drink registered a stronger brain response than the zero-calorie drink! Why does the brain's reward system react this way?

Like solving a jigsaw puzzle, these scientists eventually found their answer.

The brain's metabolic signal was responding to sweetness, and if there was a mismatch between sweetness levels and calorie levels, as happens with artificial sweeteners, the human system gets confused and pretends to metabolize calories that don't really exist in the artificial sweeteners. The result is that calories absorbed from elsewhere get stored more readily in body fat. For example, when a person consumes carbohydrates from something like potato chips, while drinking a diet soda, this facilitates a greater metabolic response and weight gain.

These findings affirmed data from previous animal studies that found animals given artificial sweeteners gained more weight than animals who didn't consume them. Not only that, but the test animals preferred consuming these artificial sweeteners more than consuming addictive drugs.

It may sound counter-intuitive to say intense sweetness can be more satisfying to the brain - and thus more addictive - than a highly addictive substance like cocaine, but that is exactly what the research shows. When given the choice of water sweetened with calorie- free saccharin, or intravenous shots of cocaine, 94% of the animals tested "preferred the sweet taste of saccharin," reported the science journal, PLoS One. "Our findings clearly demonstrate that intense sweetness can surpass cocaine reward."

You can probably imagine the implications of this finding. If most people unknowingly find artificial sweeteners to be as addictive as cocaine, and then they consume more drinks or products containing the sweeteners, they will be packing on the calories from the sugar-free food sources. Instead of losing weight with diet products, they are tricked into consuming more and gaining weight, all the while buying into advertising campaign gimmicks telling them they are doing the right thing for weight loss.

Don't you think the food scientists and marketing gurus within the processed foods industry know about this trick and exploit it - and other tricks of the trade - at every opportunity? You bet they do!

Veldhuizen MG. Et al. "Integration of Sweet Taste and Metabolism Determines Carbohydrate Reward." Curr Biol. 2017 August.
Lenoir M. et al. "Intense sweetness surpasses cocaine reward." PLoS One. 2007 August.

Addiction Tricks of Food Manufacturers

As we discussed earlier, potato chips are one of the food industry's most prized chemical creations. Let's take an even closer look at how they were designed in such a way so 'you can't eat just one.'

It's the high ratio of the fats and carbohydrates mixture (combined with salt) that helps to explain why people are so overly attracted to potato chips. In an ingenious study done with lab animals, German scientists used high-tech MRIs to peer into the brains of rats that were fed either potato chips or ordinary rat chow (the rats preferred the potato chips) and revealed how the combination of fats and carbohydrates directly stimulated the pleasure centers of the rat brains, much as happens with humans.

Further research done by scientists in Germany and Canada, using fMRI scanning on humans, affirmed "that foods high in fat and carbohydrate are, calorie for calorie, valued more than foods containing only fat or carbohydrate and that this effect is associated with greater recruitment of {the brain's} central reward circuits."

Other research from Britain found potato chips (or 'crisps' as the British call them) to be as addictive as hard drugs. Neuroscientist Tony Goldstone, of Imperial College, London, conducted a series of experiments to find out what makes people crave snack foods. He did brain scans of overweight and obese volunteers as they viewed images of potato chips and other junk food. The same brain areas were stimulated by potato chip images as were triggered in drug addicts who saw images of cocaine and in alcoholics who saw images of alcohol.

"Revealing the scientific secrets of why people can't stop after eating one potato chip." ScienceDaily. April 11, 2013. DiFeliceantonio AG. Et al. "Supra-Additive Effects of Combining Fat and Carbohydrate on Food Reward." Cell Metab. 2018 July.

One other common food substance does surpass potato chips on the addiction scale---chocolate. Knowing this fact has prompted food chemists to experiment with various combinations of the key ingredients in chocolate: sugar, cocoa, and fat. To map the human brain regions most affected by these combinations, Drexel University scientists measured the impact of each incremental increase in the chocolate's sugar content.

"We found a measurable psychoactive dose-effect relationship with each incremental increase in the chocolate's sugar content," the scientists reported, in a 2019 issue of the science journal, *Nutrients*.

> "These results suggest that each incremental increase in chocolate's sugar content enhances its psychoactive effects. These results extend our understanding of chocolate's appeal and unique ability to prompt an addictive-like eating response."

What we call 'processed' foods are basic agricultural products—like potatoes--- that have been heated and pulverized and denatured, then blended with a range of chemical additives, a process the food industry calls 'fortification' and 'enrichment.' What results are 'hyperpalatable' foods which activate the brain's pleasure circuits much more than do the less processed foods, thus making the processed ones more sought after.

These "ultra-processed foods tend to be energy-dense, low-cost, and nutrient-poor," observed the science journal, Frontiers of Nutrition, in 2019. "Ultra-processed foods contribute more than 60% of energy to diets in the U.S.," becoming a huge contributing factor to negative health outcomes, particularly obesity.

Not surprisingly, these negative health impacts of processed foods are showing up at the earliest ages of life. Brazilian scientists, in 2019, studied 307 low-income children, submitting them to blood tests and other health assessments at ages 4 and 8, and found direct evidence "that early ultra-processed food consumption played a role in increasing abdominal obesity in children."

"Proof that crisps are as addictive as hard drugs: Neuroscientists find." The Daily Mail (UK). May 20, 2017.
Casperson SL. Et al. "Increasing Chocolate's Sugar Content Enhances Its Psychoactive Effects and Intake." Nutrients. 2019 March. Gupta S. et al. "Characterizing Ultra-Processed Foods by Energy Density, Nutrient Density, and Cost." Front Nutr. 2019 May.

On average, consuming even a modest amount of ultra-processed foodstuffs each day adds at least 500 additional calories for your body to either metabolize or more probably, to store as fat, according to a 2019 study, in Cell Metabolism. **In order to lose the buildup of excess weight you will experience from absorbing those extra 500 calories a day, you must limit or totally eliminate your consumption of all ultra-processed foods.**

One of the co-authors of this calorie study, Kevin D. Hall, a scientist at the National Institute of Diabetes and Digestive and Kidney Diseases, has been involved in a related series of studies generating evidence that the 'ultra-processed' foods disrupt gut-brain signals, which are supposed to help prevent overeating by telling us when we feel satiated. These types of foods appear highly seductive because of the way industrial food formulators have manipulated the combinations of ingredients, particularly carbs, to confuse the brain and increase insulin levels in the blood. Those insulin increases alter fat cells and fat storage in the body.

In a very real sense, 'ultra-processed' foods, with all of their witch's brew combinations of fats, sugar, salt, and chemical additives, provoke cravings and as a result, these foods truly resemble addictive drugs. Like other addictions, the 'ultra-processed' food addiction requires a concerted commitment to overcome their toxic effects.

As you can now see, all of the hidden reasons for why you are becoming a body fat magnet - the soil micronutrient depletion, the hormone imbalances, sleep deprivation, chronic stress and chemical toxins exposure, and the minefield of triggers for food cravings - all together present serious challenges to the success of most dietary and weight loss plans. This is what we call a toxic synergy, and its shadowy presence in our lives makes it even more urgent for us to counteract its effects by creating self-healing lifestyle habits and health-protective strategies.

Now that we know many of the reasons why it's so easy to gain the weight - and our resulting difficulty in keeping it off - in Part Two, we examine the how of this phenomenon as it relates to the most popular dieting programs being relentlessly marketed to you.

Costa CS. Et al. "Ultra-processed food consumption and its effects on anthropometric and glucose profile: A longitudinal study during childhood." Nutra Metab Cardiovasc Dis. 2019 February.
Hall KD. Et al. "Ultra-Processed Diets Cause Excess Calorie Intake and Weight Gain: An Inpatient Randomized Controlled Trial of Ad Libitum Food Intake." Cell Metab. 2019 August.
Ellen Ruppel Shell. "A New Theory of Obesity." Scientific American. 2019 October.

Highlights

OF PART ONE

Our crop soils have become micro-nutrient deficient, which affects food crop quality and which, in turn, undermines the human metabolism controlling weight.

Hormone imbalances in both women and men often result in weight gain.

Sleep disruption (both having too little and too much sleep) encourages your body to store fat. Also, so does when we sleep play a key factor in our weight.

Chronic stress produces the hormone cortisol, which prompts your body to store abdominal fat in response; the more fat you store, the more stress you put on your body, creating a vicious cycle.

Habitual cell phone use can disrupt brain mechanisms related to metabolism control, resulting in higher caloric consumption.

Insulin resistance (insulin being the hormone that tells your body's cells to form blood sugar) results in weight gain. What triggers insulin resistance are abdominal fat, lack of exercise, and consuming highly processed foods.

Synthetic chemical toxins found in foods, clothing, and consumer products can disrupt hormones and produce weight gain. Mothers can pass these chemicals on to their child in the womb, triggering childhood obesity.

Many prescription drugs, including steroids for arthritis, can stimulate weight gain.

Many food and drink products marketed as 'diet' and 'dietary' contain artificial sweeteners that disrupt the metabolism and produce weight gain.

Food chemists and product manufacturers know how to produce food products to stimulate food cravings that create addictions and cause the overconsumption of unhealthy foods that generate weight gain.

PART TWO:

Why Diets Usually Fail You

It's human nature to rejoice in happy endings, particularly after we've been cheering for someone to succeed when the odds favor failure. That could have been one ingredient explaining the widespread popularity of the NBC reality television show, 'The Biggest Loser,' which pitted seriously overweight people against each other in a contest to see who could lose the most pounds. Some of the contestants lost several hundred unwanted pounds from a combination of strict dieting and strenuous exercise.

What eventually tempered enthusiasm for the show were unsettling revelations about what happened to most of the contestants when they went home. A team of scientists, under a grant from the National Institutes of Health, studied 14 participants from Season 8 of the show, evaluating what they experienced over the six years since they lost large amounts of weight. The study findings stamped a sobering truth across all the inflated claims made by the weight loss industry.

Within six years of being on the show, *13 of the 14* contestants who were studied had not only regained all of the weight they had worked so hard to lose, four of them actually became fatter than before their appearance on television. Their bodies seemed to have rebelled and fought back against losing so much weight so quickly.

Why did this boomerang effect happen? What the scientists discovered, through rigorous testing, was how the metabolisms of all the contestants had slowed down considerably and stayed slow following the contest, resulting in steady weight gain. Not only that but all of the contestants were found to have lower levels of the hormone leptin in their bodies - a hormone that controls appetite - creating almost constant hunger pangs, further undermining their efforts to keep weight off using dieting and exercise.

When the science team wrote up their results in a 2016 issue of the medical journal, Obesity, they observed how, in the short term, the contestants lost a substantial amount of weight thanks in part, to a support system of external accountability (sticking to set goals, combined with millions of people watching and rooting for them.) But in the long term, a wildcard factor that hadn't been anticipated turned out to be a phenomenon called metabolic adaptation, which acts to counter weight loss. In other words, the more weight you quickly lose, the more your body fights to regain it. The lesson here: lose weight slowly and consistently.

Fothergill E. Et al. "Persistent metabolic adaptation 6 years after 'The Biggest Loser' competition." Obesity. 2016 August.

This phenomenon helps to explain 'yo-yo dieting' and why most diet programs set users up for eventual failure. To illustrate what we mean, data compiled by the National Center for Health Statistics shows that in any given 12-month period, about one-half of all adults in the U.S. try to lose weight using either dieting (eating less food), increasing time spent exercising, or both. More women than men attempt to lose weight: 60% of women, 41% of men.

Among those attempting weight loss, most will not only fail, but two-thirds of them will put on more weight again than when they began dieting. This is true across diverse countries and cultures. For example, the *International Journal of Epidemiology* reported in 2011 how it found that fewer than 10% of Britain's residents succeed in losing any significant amount of weight each year, and most of them put the weight back on within a year.

When the study came out revealing what happened to contestants in 'The Biggest Loser,' the show's executive producer, JD Roth, who is credited with creating the fad of weight loss television, confessed to being perplexed and alarmed, but he nonetheless took personal action on his own. He not only changed his own diet from one of meat consumption to only consuming plant-based whole food meals, he created a book and a new six-episode television series called 'The Big Fat Truth,' in which he promoted a plant-based diet as a key to good health and weight loss. Roth credits his wife, and the research of pioneering Cornell University nutrition scientist, Dr. T. Colin Campbell, with influencing him to change his own health destiny by making more positive lifestyle decisions.

To lose weight steadily, in a healthy way - and sustain that weight loss over time - it's important to build a mindset for healthier habits to help counteract your brain's natural tendency to keep a set point for weight in place. It's been said that while your genetic gun is already loaded at birth, it's your lifestyle decisions over the decades that pull the trigger to determine your health destiny.

"Attempts to Lose Weight Among Adults in the United States, 2013-2016." National Center for Health Statistics. NCHS Data Brief # 313, July 2018.
Kuh D. Et al. "Cohort Profile: Updating the cohort profile for the MRC National Survey of Health and Development: a new clinic-based data collection for aging research." Int. J. Epidemiology. 2011.
JD Roth. "Big Fat Truth: Behind-the-Scenes Secrets to Losing Weight and Gaining the Inner Strength to Transform Your Life." 2016, Reader's Digest.

Rounding Up the Usual Diet Program Suspects

Dozens of diet plans have emerged in mainstream culture and been popularized, only to largely disappear from public view and end up mostly forgotten. New diets are being introduced all the time. A few diets which have stuck around over the past few decades and continue to be embraced by weight-conscious consumers, have received scrutiny from scientists in research trials.

25 Diets Contrasted

Atkins Diet

Cardiologist Robert C. Atkins created this low-carbohydrates eating plan in the 1960s, placing an emphasis on consuming fats and proteins while drastically restricting the intake of carbohydrates, especially refined carbs, white flour, and sugar, which lead to blood sugar imbalances and weight gain.

There are how-to books, cookbooks, and dietary products all accompanying the plan. If you go off the plan and begin eating carbs once again, you can probably expect to gain back all of the weight you lost.

While the Atkins plan claims that anyone can lose up to 15 pounds during their first two weeks on the program, it also acknowledges that most of that weight loss will be in water weight. "Most people can lose weight on most any diet plan that restricts calories - at least in the short term," observed medical specialists at The Mayo Clinic. "Over the long term, though, studies show that low-carb diets like the Atkins Diet are no more effective for weight loss than are standard weight loss diets and that most people regain the weight they lost regardless of diet plan."

Bahamian Diet

Civil Rights activist and comedian Dick Gregory created this diet (and accompanying supplement) in the 1980s to treat his own health issues and as a result, he reportedly lost more than 100 pounds. The diet itself is vegetarian and the dietary regimen also uses intermittent fasting, involving water or juices.

The diet involves using a powdered meal replacement drink (originally marketed as Formula 4X, but the name changed decades later to Dick Gregory's Caribbean Diet for Optimal Health.) Though the powder is a proprietary formula, it is said to be 100% vegan using plant protein, and can be mixed with water, almond or rice milk, coconut water, or unsweetened juice.

Gregory's original 4X powdered meal formula was tested in a study among a group of New Orleans police officers who were able to lose weight on it. (The study identified the powder's ingredients as processed sesame seed, pumpkin seeds, sunflower seed, wheat grass powder, alfalfa, acerola, date powder, carob powder, sea vegetation such as kelp, chlorophyll powder, wheat bran extract, and rice bran extract.) In the police study, 89 persons participated for up to 10 weeks, and lost an average of almost 10 pounds per person.

DASH (Dietary Approaches to Stop Hypertension) Diet

An eating plan promoted by the National Heart, Lung, and Blood Institute for lowering blood pressure, it discourages salty and fatty foods like full-fat dairy and fatty meats, but advocates fruits, vegetables, whole grains, and low-fat meat and dairy products.

Among other dietary recommendations in the plan: switch white flour to whole-wheat flour, snack on nuts instead of chips, replace salt with herbs and spices, have at least two or more meat-free meals a week, and take a 15-minute walk after each meal. The NHLBI presents several hundred recipes on its website that follow the DASH diet plan.

To assess the DASH diet's effect on body weight, the journal *Obesity Review* compared 13 studies in which the DASH diet was evaluated. On the whole, after 24 weeks, those on the diet lost more weight than people in control groups, though the amounts varied from study to study. The low-caloric DASH plan "led to even more weight reduction when compared with other low-energy diets," the study review stated.

"Atkins Diet: What's behind the claims." The Mayo Clinic Staff. https://www.mayoclinic.org/healthy-lifestyle/weight-loss/in-depth/atkins-diet/art-20048485 Lulseged S. "Clinical studies of a vegetarian food diet mixture." Journal of the National Medical Association. 1989.

Eco-Atkins Diet

Devised by researchers at St. Michael's Hospital in Toronto, this low-carb variation on the traditional Atkins Diet calls for 31 percent of daily calories to come from plant proteins, 43 percent from plant fats, and 26 percent from carbohydrates. Whereas the traditional Atkins allows meat consumption, the Eco-Atkins limits fried and processed foods, and people on it must give up eating meat and related animal products. Protein in the diet comes from plants and soy-based fake meat alternatives.

To determine the effect of this diet on weight loss and LDL cholesterol, a study in the *Archives of Internal Medicine* assessed 47 overweight hyperlipidemic men and women by dividing them into two groups for four weeks: a low-carbohydrate high vegetable protein Eco-Atkins groups and a high-carbohydrate lacto-ovo vegetarian diet group. Weight loss turned out to be similar for both diets, around eight pounds for each; however, the Eco-Atkins diet proved to have lipid-lowering advantages.

Fasting

For several thousand years fasting was primarily used in religious rituals. In the 20th century, its potential for weight loss was recognized and investigated. From juice fasts to water-only fasts, numerous applications became both trendy and the subject of clinical studies. One approach that emerged early in the 21st century became known as intermittent energy restriction, or regular periodic fasting, either every other day or once or twice a week.

In 2019, nutrition scientists at King's College London tested intermittent fasting against severe energy (caloric) restriction in 43 test subjects, who ranged in age from 35 to 75 years, and all of whom were obese. The science team defined 'intermittent fasting' as 48 hours of consuming less than 600 calories a day, followed by five days of normal eating; and 'severe energy restriction' as 500 calories a day or less consumed and done continuously over the four weeks of the study period.

What the scientists discovered after a month was that "reductions in body weight were equivalent in both groups," a mean weight loss of 2.6% of body weight for the two fasting approaches.

Alternate day fasting benefits were affirmed in a study which compared alternate day fasting combined with exercise, to either fasting on its own, or exercise on its own, to assess the weight loss benefits and the positive impact on non-alcoholic fatty liver disease, for which weight gain and obesity are documented causes. Eight adults with obesity and non-alcoholic fatty liver disease were randomized into one of four groups for a period of three months. One group did an alternate

Soltani S. et al. "The effect of dietary approaches to stop hypertension (DASH) diet on weight and body composition in adults: a systematic review and meta-analysis of randomized controlled clinical trials." Obes Rev. 2016 May.
Jenkins DJ. Et al. "The effect of a plant-based low-carbohydrate (Eco-Atkins) diet on body weight and blood lipid concentrations in hyperlipidemic subjects." Arch Intern Med. 2009 June.

day fast with moderate intensity aerobic exercise (five sessions per week, an hour each session), the second group did alternate day fasting alone, the third group did exercise alone, and the fourth group did not have any intervention. The combination of alternate day fasting and exercise significantly outperformed the other three groups in body weight loss, fat mass and waist circumference reduction, along with the benefits of improved insulin sensitivity and fatty liver healing.

GOLO Diet

GOLO as a company began in 2009 with the diet plan creation credited to a psychiatrist. In the GOLO for Life commercials seen frequently on television, several claims are made that the plan will 'put dieting behind you,' and weight loss results will last indefinitely. GOLO focuses on regulating an unbalanced hormone - insulin - which the GOLO plan says causes you to gain weight, even if you are physically active and eating healthy foods. GOLO requires you to take a special supplement and follow their eating plan to 'balance' your insulin levels, control your blood sugar, and speed up your metabolism, thus losing weight.

To follow the GOLO meal plan you must purchase educational booklets which range in price from $49.95 to $99.90, and you must purchase weight loss supplements, a pill called Release, costing up to $100 for a 90-day supply. This supplement contains magnesium, chromium, zinc, and plant extracts (such as Rhodiola root) in a proprietary formula. You take one supplement three times every day with your meals.

GOLO promotions refer to several 'preliminary' science studies that allegedly support the effectiveness of their supplements. But as *Prevention magazine* pointed out in 2022, "the studies were paid for by GOLO and cannot be found on peer-reviewed databases."

Under the GOLO diet plan, you aren't prohibited, or even otherwise restricted, from eating butter and sugars, and carbohydrates. However the plan does emphasize unprocessed foods, selecting one or two servings from fats, carbs, vegetables, and protein food groups.

Jenny Craig

Founded in 1983, as a nutrition and weight loss company, The Jenny Craig Diet emphasizes smaller meal portions and restricting calories and fat. Packaged meals are delivered to a client's door, and personal consultants are available to members, in person and via online video, for advice and motivational talks.

"Effect of alternate day fasting combined with aerobic exercise on non-alcoholic fatty liver disease: A randomized controlled trial." Ezpeleta M. Et al. Cell Metabolism. 2023 January.

Pinto AM. Et al. "Intermittent energy restriction is comparable to continuous energy restriction for cardiometabolic health in adults with central obesity: A randomized controlled trial; the Met-IER study." Clin Nutr. 2019 July.

"What Is the GOLO Diet? Why Dietitians Aren't Fans of the Pricey Weight Loss Plan." Korin Miller. Prevention. July 7, 2022. https://www.prevention.com/weight-loss/diets/a30211399/golo-diet-for-weight-loss/

"The GOLO Diet Is Built On a Pricey Pill and Little Research." Katie Dupere and Paul Kita. Men's Health. May 4, 2022. https://www.menshealth.com/nutrition/a30360542/golo-diet/

A plan member's diet can range from 1,200 to 2,300 calories daily based on the member's current weight, gender, age, fitness habits, and other factors. The program can be costly, with a $99 enrollment fee and another daily or monthly fee for the packaged foods sent by mail.

A weight loss review of published studies in 2015, compared the Jenny Craig results to Nutrisystem, Weight Watchers, and the Medifast programs. A total of 39 clinical trials were evaluated. After 12 months, Jenny Craig participants showed a 4.9% greater weight loss than control groups, Weight Watcher participants had a 2.6% greater loss than controls, Nutrisystem participants achieved a 3.8% greater weight loss, and Medifast showed a 4% loss.

Keto Diet

Though it may sound like a new dietary plan, ketogenic or 'keto' diets have been around since the 1920s, when they were first introduced as a fat-burning approach as part of the treatment for epilepsy patients. The idea behind the Keto Diet is that when you don't consume carbohydrates for extended periods, your liver begins converting your stored body fat into molecules called ketones, which will provide fuel for your body to function.

To follow the diet, you eat less than 50 grams of carbohydrates a day - which is something like a cup of pasta - and you eat a lot of fats composed of such foods as avocado, nuts, olives, cheeses, etc. In theory, this diet is designed to mimic the effect you get when fasting.

In a test of the diet's weight loss impact, scientists writing in the Annals of Internal Medicine described how they took 120 overweight adult volunteers and divided them into two groups: a low-carbohydrate diet similar to the Keto Diet, and a low-fat diet. Both test groups also undertook an exercise regimen and group motivational meetings. At 24 weeks, weight loss was almost twice as much in the low-carbohydrate group than in the low-fat study group (9.4 kg lost on average with the low-carb diet, versus 4.8 lost on average with the low-fat diet.)

A 2019 review of studies on the effectiveness of the ketogenic diet for enhancing weight loss found it to be "a potentially promising diet for reducing obesity," but also determined that "questions surrounding the sustainability of this diet for the long-term remain."

Gudzune KA. Et al. "Efficacy of commercial weight loss programs: an updated systematic review." Ann Intern Med. 2015 April.
Yancy WS. Et al. "A Low-Carbohydrate, Ketogenic Diet versus a Low-Fat Diet To Treat Obesity and Hyperlipidemia: A Randomized, Controlled Trial." Annals Int Med. 2004 May. Murphy EA. Jenkins TJ. "A ketogenic diet for reducing obesity and maintaining capacity for physical activity: hype or hope?" Curr Opin Clin Nutr Metab Care. 2019 July.

Macrobiotic Diet

Developed in the 1920s by a Japanese philosopher of Zen Buddhism, it's often described as vegetarian or even vegan, but this vegetable-rich diet does allow for some fish consumption. It emphasizes organic produce and whole grains, and there are strict rules about foods to be eaten and how they are prepared and stored.

The diet bans the use of most sugars and sweeteners, along with fruits and nuts in excess, and prohibits meat, poultry, eggs, and dairy products. Usually, whole grains, such as brown rice, barley, buckwheat, and millet, comprise half of the content of every meal. The rest of every meal is mostly composed of soups, beans, and vegetables. Chewing each bite thoroughly is emphasized.

Though the diet isn't said to be intended for weight loss, this may happen for some people because of consuming the complex carbohydrates and whole foods combination. Few clinical studies have been done on its weight loss potential, but a 2019 review of the scientific literature compared the effectiveness of six months or more on these diets: macrobiotic, vegan, vegetarian, Mediterranean, intermittent fasting, and low carbohydrate. Results indicated that the vegan and macrobiotic diets were best for glycemic control, while the Mediterranean and vegetarian diets showed greater body weight reduction.

Mediterranean Diet

It's a misnomer to think there is just one Mediterranean diet, since each country in the Mediterranean - Greece, Italy, France, etc.- have slightly different dietary habits. There are certain principles in common, however, involving components of the pattern of eating. In general, it emphasizes vegetables, whole grains, nuts, olive oil, and other healthful foods, and restricts or prohibits red meat, sugar, and saturated fat. Vigorous physical activity is important to the lifestyle, as is dining with family and friends in a relaxed atmosphere.

Can you lose weight on it? A study involving 259 overweight diabetics divided them up into three dietary groups: a low-carbohydrate Mediterranean, a traditional Mediterranean diet, and an American Diabetic Association diet. Their average age was 55 years, and they stayed on their respective assigned diet for one year. Participants in all groups were encouraged to exercise at least three times a week for 30 to 45 minutes. At the study's end, all groups lost weight, but the low-carb Mediterranean group lost an average of 22 pounds, compared to 16 pounds on average for the traditional Mediterranean, and 17 pounds on average for the ADA group.

Papamichou D. Et al. "Dietary patterns and management of type 2 diabetes: A systematic review of randomized clinical trials." Nutr Metab Cardiovasc Dis. 2019 June.

Noom

This smartphone application (app), introduced in 2013, acts as a psychological tool to help change bad eating habits as part of a weight loss strategy. The app is programmed to give feedback on food choices, and users log in their exercise routines with a built-in pedometer to track steps taken. It is based on a cognitive behavioral approach for behavior modification.

"No foods are off-limits with Noom," noted WebMD in a review of the app, though the app does make food recommendations by using color-coded food categories and provides articles about nutrition. Noom costs $59 a month and comes with access to online and text message coaches who act as behavior-change specialists.

Several medical studies have evaluated the effectiveness of Noom. A Korean study involving 35,921 overweight and obese Noom users found that three-fourths decreased their body weight over 267 days while using the app. The more users inputted their weight into the app and the more they adhered to the program, the more weight they lost. Other studies also found program adherence to be the key predictor of whether any significant weight would be lost.

Nordic Diet

Nutritional scientists at Denmark's University of Copenhagen collaborated with the co-founder of a restaurant called Noma, to create a diet based on Scandinavian culture and food traditions. It has a 2 to 1-ratio of carbohydrate grams to protein grams and involves eating less meat, using only organic produce, avoiding all food additives, and eating based on the availability of seasonal crops.

Low glycemic index foods are emphasized along with building a lifestyle around dining choices. Eating out is discouraged, but creating meals with family and friends at home is encouraged. Always eat locally produced fruits and vegetables whenever possible, and drink lots of water with every meal to aid with digestion and enhance feelings of satiety.

In a study published in the *American Journal of Clinical Nutrition*, a group of 181 obese women and men, age range 20 to 66 years, were divided into two groups: either the New Nordic Diet (high in fruit, vegetables, whole grains, and fish) or the standard Danish diet. Over 26 weeks, both groups were periodically evaluated by scientists. On average, the Nordic diet participants lost 10.3 pounds and lowered their systolic blood pressure compared to those on the standard diet.

Elhayany A. Et al. "A low carbohydrate Mediterranean diet improves cardiovascular risk factors and diabetes control among overweight patients with type 2 diabetes mellitus: a 1-year prospective randomized intervention study." Diabetes, Obesity & Met. 2010 January.
"Noom." WebMD. September 1, 2022. www.webmd.com/diet/a-z/noom-diet
Chin SO."Successful weight reduction and maintenance by using a smartphone application in those with overweight obesity." Sci Rep. 2016 November.

Nutrisystem Diet

Founded in 1972, it is one of the earliest pre-packaged home meal delivery systems and uses the glycemic index (charting how carbs affect blood sugar) as the center of its low- calorie food choices. With a focus on protein and 'good' carbs, it's intended to make users feel fuller longer while controlling their blood sugar and metabolism.

Users of the diet are encouraged to consume five or six small meals daily and the plan includes alternatives for vegetarians and diabetics. Having your meals delivered daily can be expensive, costing far more than $10 a day, though users have a wide selection of more than 100 foods to choose from.

In a 2015 study review appearing in the *Annals of Internal Medicine*, researchers compared Nutrisystem weight loss to other competing commercial weight-loss programs based on evaluating the results from 45 studies. Nutrisystem's diet was found to have resulted in a 3.8% greater weight loss at three months' use when compared to people in control groups. Though this was more weight loss than some weight loss programs, it was less loss than others.

Ornish Diet

Created in 1977 by Dr. Dean Ornish, a professor of medicine in the University of California system, the diet is low in fat, animal protein, and refined carbohydrates. Exercise (focused on aerobics and resistance training), stress management, and maintaining positive relationships are also key components of the overall dietary and weight loss program.

Though the diet was designed to help reverse heart disease, it does impact weight loss. Participants discard refined carbohydrates like pasta and white bread, avoid all saturated fats, including full-fat dairy, and stay away from most animal products and processed foods. They are encouraged to embrace meditation or other stress management techniques as part of a complete lifestyle modification.

Four weight loss diets, including Ornish, were compared in a 12-month-long clinical trial involving 311 overweight or obese premenopausal women. They were randomly assigned to either the Ornish, Atkins, Zone, or LEARN diets, and their progress was assessed at two, six, and 12-month intervals. The Atkins diet participants showed the greatest weight loss after 12 months (10.3 pounds), followed by LEARN (5.7 pounds), Ornish (4.8 pounds), and the Zone (3.5 pounds) diets respectively.

Poulsen SK. Et al. "Health effect of the New Nordic Diet in adults with increased waist circumference: a 6-mo randomized controlled trial." Am J Clin Nutr. 2013 November.
Gudzune KA. Et al. "Efficacy of Commercial Weight-Loss Programs: An Updated Systematic Review." Ann Int Med. 2015 April.

Paleo Diet

This fad diet, variously described as the caveman or stone age diet, emerged from a 1975 book by a gastroenterologist and was further refined in a 2002 book, *The Paleo Diet*. It is based on the idea that weight gain and most diseases of the 20th century have been due to processed foods and other related unhealthy dietary changes and that if we humans returned to what our ancestors ate in Paleolithic times, we could restore our health and normalize weight.

While excluding processed foods of all types, sugars and legumes, and all refined fats and carbohydrates, as well as cheese and other dairy products, the diet emphasizes the consumption of root vegetables and fruits, meats and organ meats, nuts, and eggs. Medical study results of this diet have been, at best, mixed.

A group of 70 obese postmenopausal women, average age of 60 years, joined one of two dietary groups for two years: a Nordic Nutrition Recommendations diet, or a Paleolithic- type diet. Results were measured by Swedish public health scientists and published in the *European Journal of Clinical Nutrition*. Both groups "significantly decreased total fat mass at 6 months and 24 months," the science team reported. But the Paleo participants lost 14 pounds on average at six months, compared to 6 pounds for the Nordic group. Waist circumference decreased in the Paleo group by 11.1 centimeters at 6 months, compared to 5.8 cm on the Nordic diet. In the second year of the study, however *(and this is an important point)*, both groups regained a good portion of the weight they had lost.

Gardner CD. Et al. "Comparison of the Atkins, Zone, Ornish, and LEARN diets for change in weight and related risk factors among premenopausal women: the A to Z Weight Loss Study: a randomized trial." JAMA. 2007 March.
Mellberg C. Et al. "Long-term effects of a Paleolithic-type diet in obese postmenopausal women: a2-year randomized trial." Eur J Clin Nutr. 2014 March.

Raw Food Diet

By eating only raw and living plant foods, without cooking, you are on a guaranteed path to lose weight while promoting optimal health. That is not just a finding from our seven decades of experience at Hippocrates Wellness, though *you will find more about our experiences and observations in Part III of this book.* There is independent research backing our assertions in this regard, results we believe are largely due to the much higher macro and micro-nutrient contents of organic, uncooked plant foods.

German nutritional scientists followed and assessed 216 men and 297 women for 3.7 years as they consumed a raw foods diet. The study yielded clear results that a raw food diet produces a "high loss of body weight," wrote the researchers. The regimen also enabled consumers of the diet to keep excess weight off in the long term. On average, during the study period, men lost an average of 21 pounds, and women lost an average of 26 pounds.

No other diet can match these weight losses and long-term benefits! Please note, eating raw meat IS NOT a part of our raw food diet.

_{Koebnick C. Et al. "Consequences of a long-term raw food diet on body weight and menstruation: results of a questionnaire survey." Ann Nutr Metab. 1999.}

SlimFast Diet

Started in 1977, in Florida, as a dietary supplement company, SlimFast introduced flavored diet shakes as a meal replacement and then began offering a low-calorie product line of meal bars and other snacks. The diet plan calls for eating six meals a day: including one 500-calorie meal for women, an 800-calorie meal for men, consuming two shakes or smoothies, and three 100-calorie snacks during the day.

Calories are restricted on this diet, but no specific foods are prohibited or discouraged. While it is easy to follow and less expensive than most other commercial meal plans, its products are heavily processed and there isn't educational support for encouraging healthy eating habits.

Writing in the science journal, *Obesity*, a team of scientists described a 12-month study they did with 113 obese adolescents who were assigned to either meal replacements (three SlimFast shakes, one prepackaged meal, and five vegetable/fruit servings a day) or a meal plan that restricted calorie intake to less than 1500 a day. At month four of the study, participants in the SlimFast trial had reduced their body mass index by an average of 6.3% compared to 3.8% in the other eating group. But while the use of SlimFast "significantly improved short-term weight loss," reported the scientists, *"its continued use did not improve maintenance of lost weight."*

South Beach Diet

A celebrity physician launched this diet with a bestselling book in 2003, creating a rating system for 'good' and 'bad' fats and carbohydrates. No calorie counting is involved with this low-carb diet, which defines 'good' carbs as those low in the glycemic index. Participants are encouraged to eat eggs, dairy, and lean protein like turkey and chicken, along with whole grains, nuts, and vegetables.

It is a home delivery meal program costing around $300 a month, for which subscribers receive three meals a day. It became a Keto-friendly program in 2019, carrying five dozen related products. It includes an exercise program to support the eating plan.

Independent clinical trial studies to support the ability of the South Beach Diet to shed pounds in either the short or long term are almost nonexistent. A study review in the science journal, *Nutrition*, argued that the diet's very design prevents long-term successful weight loss. Dietary fiber intake helps prevent obesity by promoting satiation and altering secretion of gut hormones, argued the study review, and "the average fiber intake of adults in the United States is less than half recommended levels and is lower still among those who follow currently popular low-carbohydrate diets such as South Beach."

Berkowitz RI. Et al. "Meal replacements in the treatment of adolescent obesity: a randomized controlled trial." Obesity. 2011 June.

Therapeutic Lifestyle Changes Diet

Created by a cholesterol education program run by the National Institutes of Health, these dietary guidelines involve sticking to a target calorie level, such as 2,500 calories a day for men and 1,800 calories daily for women. The emphasis is on vegetable consumption, fruits, breads, cereals and pasta.

Off-limits are high-fat dairy such as butter, fatty meats, and any saturated fats that are high in cholesterol. Sample meal plans are available to help consumers count the calories and stick to low-cholesterol goals. Though the diet wasn't designed for weight loss, it has been used by some consumers to advance that goal while improving their cholesterol levels.

There is little research to prove the weight loss benefits of this diet. But in a study comparing an Atkin's-like low carbohydrate diet with a TLC low-fat diet, 120 overweight people were randomized into one of the diets for six months. At the study's end, the low-carb Atkins dieters lost an average of 31 pounds, compared to an average loss of 20 pounds for the TLC low-fat dieters. Those are large sum losses, but the caveat is there was no evidence dieters were able to keep this weight off for any substantial length of time beyond the study period.

Slavin JS. "Dietary fiber and body weight." Nutrition. 2005 March.
Yancy WS. Et al. "A Low-Carbohydrate, Ketogenic Diet versus a Low-Fat Diet to Treat Obesity and Hyperlipidemia: A Randomized, Controlled Trial." Ann Int Med. 2004 May.

Vegan Diet

By removing all meat and dairy products from your diet, you will lose weight and help to protect yourself against heart disease, diabetes, and cancer. That statement is based on the findings of many dozens of medical studies conducted over the past few decades (also see our series of three books, *Food IS Medicine*, using hundreds of scientific studies to verify the health benefits - including weight loss - of totally removing meat and dairy products from your diet.)

To determine the effect of plant-based diets on weight loss, scientists at the University of South Carolina did a five-month clinical trial of overweight adults, ages 18 to 65 years, by dividing them into five eating groups: a vegan, vegetarian, pesco-vegetarian (includes fish consumption), semi-vegetarian, and omnivorous (meat eating.) At the end of six months, the vegan participants had greater weight loss than all of the other groups: a 7.5% average loss for vegans, significantly more than the 3.2% and less for the other groups.

Turner-McGrievey GM. Et al. "Comparative effectiveness of plant-based diets for weight loss: a randomized controlled trial of five different diets." Nutrition. 2015 February.

Reliance on a plant-based diet can be tailored to cultural habits and traditions, as evidenced by weight loss findings for African-Americans. Released in early 2023, this study ranks as one of the first ever designed specifically to create a "culturally-tailored plant-based nutrition and lifestyle intervention designed to improve cardiovascular risk among Black adults in a rural, Black Belt community." Participants were 24 African-Americans, average age of 43 years, living in rural Georgia.

Over 12 weeks the researchers conducted weekly educational sessions, cooking lessons, exercise and provision of individual plant-based food items and plant-based alternatives to meat and dairy products. Average body mass index and waist circumference shrank by 10.8% and both total and low-density lipoprotein cholesterol decreased by 13.9% during the 12 weeks, showing that significant weight loss and improved cardiovascular health can be achieved using a plant-based diet tailored to cultural eating habits and preferences. Concluded the research team: "We demonstrated the feasibility of introducing plant-based foods into a cultural environment where meat plays a dominant role in the diet. Our study also highlighted the importance of incorporating culturally relevant foods in lifestyle interventions."

Vegetarian Diet

Vegetarians consume fewer calories than meat eaters and as a result, they usually weigh less, too. This is a generally acknowledged truism that's backed by a wealth of scientific evidence, though the weight loss experienced on this diet is less than what vegans and raw food consumers can claim.

While there is a subcategory of eaters known as pesco-vegetarians, which means they periodically eat fish but not land animals, we are dealing here with strict vegetarians. They may consume dairy products, but they don't eat animals or fish of any kind.

Scientists from universities in Spain and Denmark followed the dietary histories of 11,554 people over a 10-year period. Over that long period of time, those who ate a vegetarian diet of healthy plant foods conferred on themselves a much-reduced long-term risk of becoming overweight or obese. No such trend for weight maintenance was found in those persons who ate meat or who consumed less-healthy plant-derived foods that had gone through processing, such as refined grains or fruit juices.

"Effect of a Plant-based Intervention Among Black Individuals in the Deep South: A Pilot Study." Sterling SR. Bowen SA. Journal of Nutrition, Education and Behavior. 2023 January.
Turner-McGrievy GM. Et al. "Comparative effectiveness of plant-based diets for weight loss: a randomized controlled trial of five different diets." Nutrition. 2015 February.

Volumetrics Diet

This diet is filling, and nothing is off-limits if you like fruits, veggies, and soups. Developed by a Penn State nutrition professor, Barbara Rolls, the idea behind it is that cutting the energy density of the foods will help you to consume fewer calories while still feeling satiated. You lose weight in the long term by feeling fuller on fewer calories consumed.

Rolls recommends eating three meals and two snacks each day, mostly fruits and vegetables, because of their stomach-filling water content. She divides the foods we eat into four categories: **(1)** *'eat anytime' fruits and vegetables and broth-based soups;* **(2)** *modest portions of whole grains, legumes, low-fat dairy and lean meats;* **(3)** *small portions of breads, cheeses, and fat-free baked goods; and finally,* **(4)** *in small amounts, nuts, and fats and fried foods.* Exercise is also recommended along with keeping a food journal.

To evaluate the energy density approach to weight loss, German and Polish scientists reviewed the results of 13 studies conducted among more than three thousand people, aged 18 to 66 years. They described how they found "a significant association between low energy density foods and body weight reductions when low energy density foods were eaten…{it} is a simple but effective measure to manage weight in the obese with the aim of weight reduction."

Wild Diet

Wild Diet creator Abel James, a musician and celebrity coach, asks: "Can you *really* lose fat while enjoying sirloin steak, chicken parmesan, chocolate, and real butter?" His answer is yes. Launched in 2015, this low-carb, high-fat diet (which James promotes as a lifestyle) resembles the Paleo Diet in the foods that are recommended.

This diet recommends avoiding processed foods while prioritizing the intake of proteins and fats, such as whole eggs, full-fat cheeses and butter, grass-fed steak, pasture-raised pork and chicken and turkey, and wild-caught salmon, sea bass, shrimp, oysters, crab, and other seafood. Users are urged to avoid whole grains, beans, lentils, and potatoes.

The closest thing to a clinical study of The Wild Diet involved a semi-comparable low-carbohydrate diet that was tested on 148 obese adults in a 12-month trial and compared to a low-fat diet. On average low-carbohydrate participants experienced about five pounds more of weight loss (if they had good adherence to the program) than test subjects who were on the low-fat diet regimen.

Gomez-Donoso C. Et al. "A Provegetarian Food Pattern Emphasizing Preference for Healthy Plant-Derived Foods Reduces the Risk of Overweight/Obesity in the SUN Cohort." Nutrients. 2019 July.

WW Diet (formerly Weight Watchers)

Weight Watchers lets you eat what you want but does require you to keep track of the point values of the foods you eat. A SmartPoints grading system assigns a point value, based on the WW Diet nutrition assessment, for every beverage or food, amounting to hundreds of foods and beverages altogether. The system is tailored to every person's current weight, gender, height, and age.

Thousands of recipes are offered in this diet, along with its database from which to calculate your daily points value, ingredient by ingredient. New members pay an initiation fee and then can sign up for monthly digital support services, workshops, and even personal coaching to meet their weight loss goals.

A review of studies evaluating commercial weight loss programs, including WW, published in 2015 by the *Annals of Internal Medicine*, found that WW participants lost 2.6% more weight over 12 months than people in control groups. But by contrast, Jenny Craig diet participants lost 4.9% more weight at 12 months than controls, and Nutrisystem dieters had a 3.8% more weight loss than controls in those studies. In other words, WW was less effective in taking weight off over a year compared to many of its competitors.

Zone Diet

Calories are restricted on this diet, as conceived by biochemist Barry Sears, to focus on the nutrient balance of having frequent meals (eating five times a day, based on three meals and two snacks) and composed of a general ratio of 40 percent carbs, 30 percent proteins, and 30 percent healthy fat. The idea is to keep inflammation stimulating hormones and insulin in a 'zone,' not too low, not too high, since Sears believes inflammation is responsible for much of the weight gain people in developed countries experience.

Generally, this diet limits women to 1,200 calories daily and men to 1,500 calories, about two-thirds of the calorie consumption recommended by mainstream medicine. It is strongly recommended that users of the diet avoid pasta, bread, potatoes, cereals, fatty red meats, egg yolks, and all processed foods. To keep blood sugar stabilized, the diet recommends never going more than five hours without consuming some food, being careful to choose low glycemic index carbohydrates.

In a 2014 *Journal of the American Medical Association* comparative review of studies examining the diet and contrasting it to other low-carbohydrate diets, some differences in weight loss between the Zone and Atkins diets were found. Six months after testing, volunteers on the Atkins diet achieved 3.7 pounds on average more weight loss than test subjects on the Zone diet. At 12 months and beyond, those differences in weight loss between the two plans narrowed depending on the user's commitment to exercise and behavioral support factors.

Gudzune KA. Et al. "Efficacy of commercial weight-loss programs: an updated systematic review." Ann Intern Med. 2015 April.
Johnston BC. Et al. "Comparison of weight loss among named diet programs in overweight and obese adults: a meta-analysis." JAMA. 2014 September.

Revisiting Weight Loss Among Popular Plans

> It's useful to spotlight science studies that contrast findings about the relative pros and cons of the various popular diet plans, as this gives us a starting point for evaluating not only their weight loss potential in the short term, but their potential failings in the long-term at keeping the weight off

In a 12-month clinical trial involving 311 overweight and obese premenopausal women, aged 25 to 50 years, the volunteers were randomly assigned to one of four diets: Atkins, Zone, Ornish, or LEARN (Lifestyle, Exercise, Attitudes, Relationships, Nutrition.)

Progress assessments were made of all participants at months 2, 6 and 12, with weight loss measured along with body fat percentage, waist-to-hip ratio, blood pressure, fasting insulin and glucose levels, and lipid profile.

"The amount of weight loss at 12 months relative to baseline {when the study began} among all groups was modest at 2% to 5%," the study team from Stanford University Medical School concluded. Among the four diets, those on the Atkins plan experienced twice the weight loss after a year (10.3 pounds on average) than any of the other plans produced.

Gardner CD. Et al. "Comparison of the Atkins, Zone, Ornish, and LEARN diets for change in weight and related risk factors among overweight premenopausal women: the A To Z Weight Loss Study: a randomized trial." JAMA. 2007 March.

A 2017 survey of results from clinical trial studies of weight loss from seven popular U.S. diets - Atkins, DASH, Glycemic-Index, Mediterranean, Ornish, Paleolithic, and Zone - found "the Atkins Diet showed the most evidence in producing clinically meaningful short-term (six months) and long-term (one year) weight loss," wrote the University of Florida researchers.

However, studies tracking the longer-term (24 months and more) adherence to the Atkins and other diets found "that weight loss is partially regained over time," concluded an American Heart Association study review. The Atkins diet was only marginally more effective in keeping excess weight off in the long term. This inability to keep the weight off is the Achilles Heel of nearly all widely used diets.

There is another rarely reported factor we must keep in mind when evaluating contrasts between the various diet programs. Some of the data showing weight loss in studies may be unintentionally exaggerated, especially when it comes to tracking long-term results.

UCLA professors of psychology analyzed the results of 31 long-term studies of weight loss using popular diets. "We found that the majority of people regained all the weight, plus more. Sustained weight loss was found only in a small minority of participants, while complete regain was found in the majority. Diets do not lead to sustained weight loss for the majority of people," commented study co-author, Traci Mann.

Certain factors were found to be "biased diet studies to make them appear more effective than they really were," said Professor Mann. Because many study participants reported their results to researchers by mail or phone, instead of having their weight measured on a scale by the independent investigators, weight results tended to be skewed in favor of recording more loss than actually occurred.

A second problem with many of the studies examining weight plans was very low follow-up rates. Usually, the rates of follow-up, checking on how much weight loss was sustained, were lower in 50% of participants, which can further skew the perception of how effective a diet might be.

"People who gain back large amounts of weight are generally unlikely to show up for follow-up tests," observed Professor Mann. But it was also true that study participants who reported engaging in the most consistent exercise regimens were also the ones who experienced the greatest weight loss over long periods of time, once again showing how the consistency of exercise is related to keeping weight off.

Anton SD. Et al. "Effects of Popular Diets without Specific Calorie Targets on Weight Loss Outcomes: Systematic Review of Findings from Clinical Trials." Nutrients. 2017 July. Atallah R. Et al. "Long-term effects of 4 popular diets on weight loss and cardiovascular risk factors: a systematic review of randomized controlled trials." Circ Cardiovasc Qual Outcomes. 2014 November.
"Dieting Does Not Work, UCLA Researchers Report." UCLA Newsroom. April 3, 2007.

How cost-effective are the various weight loss strategies?

To answer that question, the science journal, *Clinical Obesity,* published a study in 2019, examining the cost-effectiveness (money spent per pound lost) of 10 weight loss interventions. Six of them were pharmaceutical products (Alli, Xenical, Qsymia, Contrave, Belviq, and Saxenda), two were lifestyle modification programs (Weight Watchers Meetings and Online) one was the food replacement program Jenny Craig, and finally, an intragastric balloon system called Orbera.

This cost comparison revealed that only Weight Watchers Meetings seemed to be cost-effective for non-surgical weight loss. The other options were priced too high to be considered cost-effective. In fact, according to this study, "for the medications to become incrementally cost-effective, *costs would have to decrease by as much as 91%."*

Another Achilles Heel flaw in most diets revolves around the nutritional quality of the food items approved for inclusion in the diet programs.

Mann T. Et al. "Medicare's search for effective obesity treatments: diets are not the answer." Ann Psychol. 2007 April.
Finkelstein EA. Verghese NR. "Incremental cost-effectiveness of evidence-based non-surgical weight loss strategies." Clin Obes. 2019 April.

Popular Diets Are Micronutrient Deficient

Earlier in this book, we described how micronutrient deficiencies appearing in our soils over the past half-century end up producing micronutrient deficiencies in many of our most common food crops. Compounding this situation is the finding that many of the most popular diet plans embraced by dieters are also highly deficient in numerous micronutrients needed to lose weight, especially in the long-term, and protect their health against disease.

In an analysis of four popular diet plans - *the Atkins for Life* low carbohydrate diet, the *Atkins for Life Mediterranean* style plan, *The South Beach Diet,* and the *DASH* (Dietary Approaches to Stop Hypertension) low-fat diet plan - foods used in each daily meal plan had their levels of 27 essential micronutrients assessed and the calorie content calculated. The micronutrient levels in each diet were compared to amounts suggested for adults, between the ages of 18 and 55 years, by the U.S. Food and Drug Administration.

According to the findings, published in the Journal of the *International Society of Sports Nutrition*, all four diet plans were deficient in a majority of the 27 essential micronutrients. Both of the Atkins diets were missing a dozen micronutrients in sufficient amounts to support health; The South Beach Diet was missing 21 in health-necessary levels, and the DASH diet was found deficient in 13 micronutrients.

On average, the four diet plans contained only:

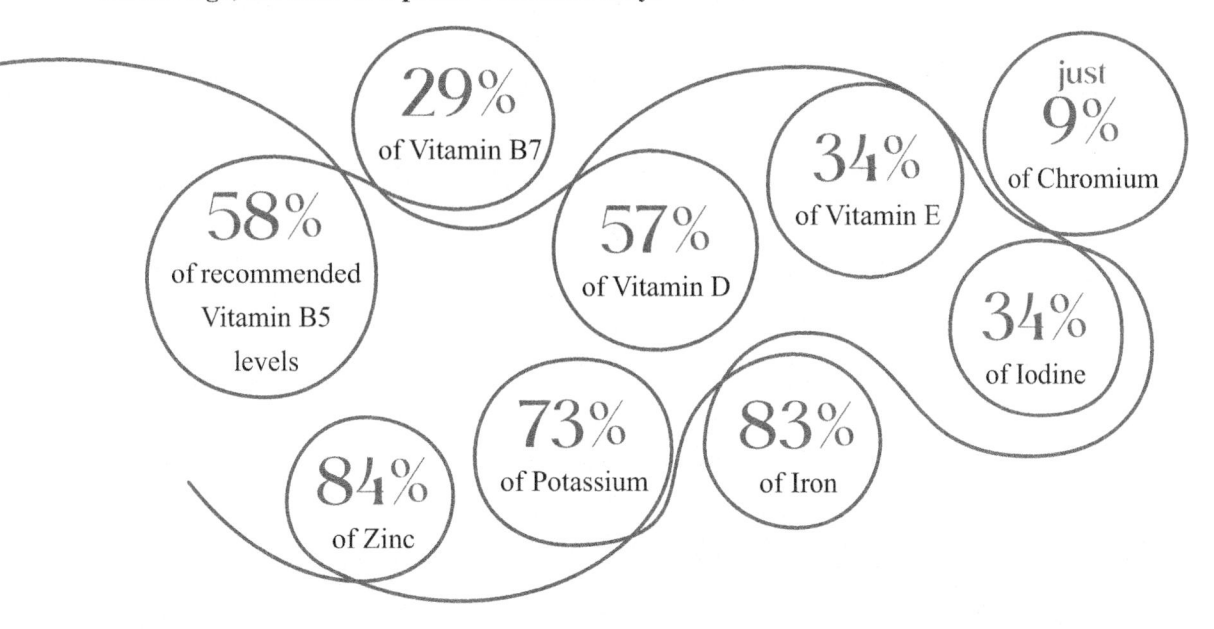

- 58% of recommended Vitamin B5 levels
- 29% of Vitamin B7
- 57% of Vitamin D
- 34% of Vitamin E
- just 9% of Chromium
- 34% of Iodine
- 84% of Zinc
- 73% of Potassium
- 83% of Iron

In order to raise the daily micronutrient intake, while remaining within the parameters for each of the diet plans, calorie consumption would need to be elevated to almost ridiculous levels. It was calculated that the *Atkins for Life diet*, for example, would *require consuming 37,500 calories daily* for a person to become 100% sufficient in micronutrients. That would be "well over any calorie intake levels in which weight loss and/or health benefits could be achieved," wrote the study authors. It's fair to say these micronutrient deficiencies undermine the entire stated intentions and premise of the diets to help achieve healthy weight loss.

"The implications of this study are significant and far-reaching," continued the scientists assessing their results. "Micronutrient deficiency has been shown to cause an 80.8% increase in the likelihood of becoming overweight or obese and is scientifically linked to a higher risk of other dangerous and debilitating diseases, including resistance to infection, birth defects, cancer, cardiovascular disease and osteoporosis…{for anyone following one of these four diet plans}…micronutrient deficiency is inevitable."

We would like to see similar micronutrient assessments done for all of the various dietary plans mentioned in this book. **If we were to hazard a guess, based on the available scientific literature, the only dietary regimens coming close to meeting or exceeding nutrient guidelines would be the vegan diet and the one we champion, raw living foods!**

Calton JB."Prevalence of micronutrient deficiency in popular diet plans." J Int Soc Sports Nutr. 2010 June.

Why a Vegan Diet Equals Weight Loss

As indicated earlier, in contrasting the various diets, by following a vegan dietary regimen - no meat, no dairy, no animal products - a vast body of scientific literature has emerged showing a range of health benefits, most particularly in the loss of weight. Only a raw living foods diet eclipses it.

A group of 30 obese children were divided up into two groups: one followed a vegan diet for four weeks, the other group ate a diet recommended by the American Heart Association (AHA), which consisted of more protein and saturated fat than the vegan diet.

At the end of the four-week study, children on the vegan diet lost an average of 6.7 pounds, which was 197% more lost weight than those in the AHA dietary group. The vegan group also had a significantly lower body mass index than the AHA group, and lower total and LDL cholesterol levels, as well as lower systolic blood pressure and blood sugar levels.

A 2015 study, published in the journal, *Nutrition,* worked with 50 overweight adults, aged 18 to 65 years, who had been divided into five groups: vegan, vegetarian, pesco-vegetarian (someone who adds fish or seafood to a vegetarian diet), semi-vegetarian, or omnivorous. For six months, the study participants were encouraged to stick to their assigned diet plans; the only thing they did in common was to take a daily vitamin B12 supplement.

Macknin M et al. "Plant-Based, No-Added-Fat or American Heart Association Diets: Impact on Cardiovascular Risk in Obese Children with Hypercholesterolemia and Their Parents. The Journal of Pediatrics. 2015.

After six months, the vegan dieters had lost 7.5% of their body weight, which was more than twice the weight loss of any of the other four dietary groups. The research team from the University of South Carolina was able to declare the vegan diet to be the most effective weight loss option for overweight people to pursue.

Finally, and convincingly, a team of scientists writing in the *European Journal of Clinical Nutrition* described how they recruited 291 adults working in the offices of a large insurance company, and placed them on either a vegan diet or a control diet that didn't involve dietary changes, over an 18-week period.

Not only did the vegan dieters lose an average of 9.5 pounds compared to no loss in the control group, the vegan group improved their blood cholesterol and blood sugar levels, along with blood pressure, compared to no change in the control group.

As for micronutrient intake and a vegan diet, Swiss scientists did an analysis in 2017, using a group of test subjects who were omnivores or vegans and measuring their intake of several dozen micronutrients. As expected, omnivores had deficiencies in numerous micronutrients, ranging from magnesium to folic acid. Vegetarians also had numerous deficiencies, such as vitamin B6 and niacin, though much less than the omnivores. By contrast, vegans were only deficient in vitamin B12, which could easily be remedied using supplements.

If you are someone who has experimented with short-cuts, turning to weight loss drugs as an alternative to dieting, or doing so because the diets you tried didn't work as hoped, information in the following section of the book probably won't surprise you.

Turner-McGrievy GM. Et al. "Comparative effectiveness of plant-based diets for weight loss: a randomized controlled trial of five different diets. Nutrition. 2015 February. Mishra S. et al. "A multicenter randomized controlled trial of a plant-based nutrition program to reduce body weight and cardiovascular risk in the corporate setting: the GEICO study. Eur J Clin Nutr. 2013.
Schupbach R. Et al. "Micronutrient status and intake in omnivores, vegetarians and vegans in Switzerland." European J Nutrition. 2017 February.

How Safe and Affordable are Weight Loss Drugs?

Rather than diet or exercise, many people turn to prescription weight loss drugs for 'a quick fix' attempt to shed pounds. Adverse reactions to drugs designed for inducing weight loss are legendary for how alarming and persistent the side effects can be. Starting decades ago, with the use of amphetamines as an appetite suppressant, both physical and psychological health events documented by the medical industry resulted in many of the drugs being outlawed by the government.

"The most publicized of these withdrawals was for the combination of fenfluramine and phentermine ('fen-phen') and its cousin dexfenfluramine (Redux)," reported the Cleveland *Clinic Journal of Medicine,* in 2017. "Up to 30% of patients taking fenfluramine-phentermine developed echocardiographic evidence of valvular heart disease. Fenfluramine also increased the risk of pulmonary hypertension. These findings led to the 1997 withdrawal of these drugs from the US market."

In the same year as these withdrawals, a new drug, Sibutramine (marketed as Meridia) was approved for use in weight loss by the US Food and Drug Administration. After its release, a post-marketing study "found increased rates of nonfatal myocardial infarction and stroke in patients with preexisting cardiovascular disease or diabetes mellitus. Based on these results, sibutramine was withdrawn from both US and European markets."

Still another weight loss drug, Rimonabant (marketed under the brand names Acomplia and Zimulti) a cannabinoid-receptor inhibitor, "was approved in Europe in 2006, but its approval was withdrawn just two years later because of increased suicidality. It was never approved for use in the United States."

Bersoux S. et al. "Pharmacotherapy for obesity: What you need to know." Cleveland Clinic Journal of Medicine. 2017 December. Ibid.

As of 2019, a total of five weight loss drugs have been approved for sale in the U.S.- liraglutide (acts by increasing satiety and reducing food intake), lorcaserin (regulates serotonin), naltrexone/bupropion (reduces energy intake), orlistat (helps the intestines to block absorption of fat), and phentermine/topiramate (appetite suppressants).

Though all five drugs have been shown to induce modest weight loss in the short-term clinical trials that have been conducted, their long-term safety and effects on overall health remain an open question. All of these five drug weight loss options, according to a 2017 study in the science journal, *Obesity Research & Clinical Practice,* "have associated adverse events requiring long-term safety data."

Beware of weight loss supplement reliance. Many dieters rely on synthetic oral nutrition supplements to manage weight loss and in doing so, they reduce their intake of plant-sourced foods. Most of these supplements are ultra-processed and their long-term effectiveness and safety may be in doubt. A 2023 study published in early, in *Nutrition Clinical Practice,* made a case for how the effectiveness of these supplements is not only "mixed and the potential health risks of consuming ultra-processed weight loss supplements long-term have received little attention."

According to the European Society of Endocrinology, in a 2015 weight loss drug appraisal, drugs such as "lorcaserin and combinations of bupropion-naltrexone or phentermine- topiramate have not been approved in many countries {outside of the U.S.} because of safety concerns." Corona G. et al. "Body composition, metabolism and Testosterone." European Society of Endocrinology. 2015.

A 2016 study of naltrexone/bupropion and its use in 8,910 overweight, obese patients, published in the *Journal of the American Medical Association,* determined that "the cardiovascular safety of this treatment remains uncertain."

So, the continuing long-term safety concerns should give anyone considering their use reason to think long and hard about the wisdom of starting these regimens. Something else to keep in mind is that their use is intended to be part of a lifestyle modification program in which diet and exercise continue to play central roles in achieving weight loss goals. In that respect, weight loss drugs are an adjunct approach, not a 'magic bullet' substitute, for a healthy diet and an exercise routine.

"Recommending ultra-processed oral nutrition supplements for unintentional weight loss: Are there risks?" Rivero-Mendoza D. Et al. Nutr Clinical Practice 2023 February. Ibid. Cohen JB. Gadde KM. "Weight Loss Medications in the Treatment of Obesity and Hypertension." Curr Hypertens Rep. 2019 February. Hocking S. et al. "Current and emerging pharmacotherapies for obesity in Australia." Obes Res Clin Pract. 2017 September-October.
Nissen SE. Et al. "Effect of Naltrexone-Bupropion on Major Adverse Cardiovascular Events in Overweight and Obese Patients with Cardiovascular Risk Factors: A Randomized Clinical Trial." JAMA. 2016 March. Johnson G. Oliver MN. American Family Physician. Dec. 15, 2014. https://www.aafp.org/afp/2014/1215/p863.html

Lastly, these drugs can be expensive for the ordinary person. For example, lorcaserin costs around $213 for a 30-day supply (about $2,600 a year) compared to phentermine/ topiramate $160 for a 30-day supply (around $2,000 a year.) Orlistat is even more costly at from $621 to $725 for 90 capsules, or almost $3,000 annually.

Instead of prescription weight loss drugs, maybe you've tried to rely on weight loss supplements (natural or synthetic) to substitute for diets and exercise or to compensate for micronutrient deficiencies. You may then have faced the following quandary.

Johnson G. Oliver MN. American Family Physician. Dec. 15, 2014. https://www.aafp.org/afp/2014/1215/p863.html

Challenging Weight Loss Supplement Purity

While we do recommend some natural organic supplements to help with weight loss and healthy weight maintenance, we also urge caution in choosing which supplements to buy and use.

In a 2016 study, funded by the French National Agency for the Safety of Medicines and Health Products, scientists analyzed the ingredients in 160 weight loss food supplements labeled as being from 100% natural compounds, marketed in European countries. Using a highly sophisticated spectroscopy machine, they were able to identify and measure the presence of adulterants added to the alleged natural source supplements.

What the scientists discovered was nothing short of alarming. Of the 160 types of supplements, all of which claimed to be 'natural,' 56% were tainted with six active pharmaceutical ingredients. These included the prescription only weight loss drugs sibutramine and phenolphthalein, along with sildenafil, fluoxetine, and lorcaserin. Many of the supplement samples contained combinations of two or more of these pharmaceuticals.

Under European law, pharmaceutical ingredients at any level are banned from food supplements, and weight loss drugs are available by prescription only. The tainted supplements were being sold via the Internet and in some health stores and a few pharmacies.

Hachem R. et al. "Proton NMR for detection, identification and quantification of adulterants in 160 herbal food supplements marketed for weight loss." Journal of Pharmaceutical and Biomedical Analysis. 2016 May.

"The players who supply such products are essentially pirate operators who exploit the vulnerability of individuals keen to lose weight," Robert Verkerk, scientific director of the Alliance for Natural Health International, commented on the study results. "they unfortunately risk tarnishing the reputation of the vast majority of operators who maintain rigorous quality control standards."

One of our books, *Supplements Exposed,* delves into greater detail about the specifics of this unsettling and hazardous situation.

Ibid.

Why Exercise Fails to Keep Excess Weight Off

Does this statement sound familiar: So long as you exercise long enough and vigorously enough, it doesn't matter what you eat because you can always burn off those additional calories with exercise! Corporate food companies have used this refrain in their marketing pitches for unhealthy fatty foods, as have some of the weight loss plans that want you to believe you can eat whatever you want and still lose weight, if only you are active enough to burn those calories.

Science evidence tells another, more nuanced story about the role of exercise in healthy weight maintenance. While there are many reasons to regularly exercise - from developing cardiorespiratory fitness to supporting the immune system - any emphasis on weight loss from exercise requires us to carefully peek behind the curtain of claims about what physical activity will or won't do for us.

In a 2003 study, published in the *Journal of the American Medical Association,* results seemed to show that a higher duration and intensity of exercise might improve long-term weight loss. With 201 sedentary and overweight women, average age of 37 years, as test subjects, researchers assigned them to one of four exercise groups: **(1)** *vigorous intensity and high duration* **(2)** *moderate intensity and high duration* **(3)** *moderate intensity and moderate duration* **(4)** *or vigorous intensity and moderate duration.* All of the women in all the groups were asked to reduce their intake of energy (calories) to between 1200 and 1500 calories a day.

After 12 months on these exercise regimens, weight loss occurred in all four groups of women, ranging from 6.3 pounds in the moderate intensity/moderate duration group, to 8.9 pounds in the vigorous intensity/high duration group. In short, there wasn't much difference in weight loss among the four groups. (Average cardiorespiratory fitness also increased significantly in all four groups, but with no statistically significant difference between the groups.)

In their conclusions, the scientists wrote: "Significant weight loss and improved cardiorespiratory fitness were achieved through the combination of exercise and diet during 12 months, although *no differences were found* based on different exercise durations and intensities in this group of sedentary, overweight women."

We find these outcomes important for several reasons. First, the study capped out at 12 months, and so no long-term follow-up was done to see how many of these women kept the weight off. (Our guess is that few of them did.) Second, while all four groups were asked to limit their daily caloric intake, no scrutiny was given to the *quality of their diets* to gauge whether they were absorbing adequate amounts of micronutrients. Both of these factors could play roles in influencing or exaggerating differences in the outcomes of the four exercise routines and whether the weight loss was simply transitory.

We know that regular exercise, irrespective of intensity or duration, is one of the keys to moderating the metabolic adaptations that the body uses to promote rapid and efficient weight regain after weight loss. This point became clear in research conducted at the University of Colorado, Denver, where researchers in the Center for Human Nutrition, Department of Medicine, tested animals on treadmills to measure the extent of the impact on weight regain.

The test animals were first placed on a 16-week fat-feeding diet that made them obese, and then placed on a calorie-restricted, low-fat diet for eight weeks until they lost 14% of their body weight. After that, they worked out on a regular treadmill exercise routine while their physiology was monitored. Reported the science team: "Regular exercise decreased the rate of {weight} regain…and…reduced the biological drive to eat." It was clear that the regular exercise (not the intensity of it) helped to alter the body's metabolic adaptations that would have otherwise caused the animals to regain the lost weight.

If you have stopped exercising for any period of time, you probably know how difficult it is to shed those pounds you put on during your hiatus. Scientists at the Berkeley Lab's Life Sciences Division surveyed the exercise routines of thousands of men and women and found that exercise must be regular the year round, because quitting results in gaining weight that the human body becomes resistant to losing again.

Jakicic JM. Et al. "Effect of exercise duration and intensity on weight loss in overweight, sedentary women: a randomized trial." JAMA. 2003 September.
MacLean PS. Et al. "Regular exercise attenuates the metabolic drive to regain weight after long-term weight loss." Am J Physiol Regul Integr Comp Physiol. 2009 September.

"The price to pay for quitting exercise is higher than expected, and this price may be an important factor in the obesity epidemic affecting Americans," observed study co-author Paul Williams. "In other words, if you stop exercising, you don't get to resume where you left off if you want to lose weight."

A key finding that led to his conclusion came from noticing that people who decreased their running distance from five to zero miles per week gained four times as much weight as people who decreased their running distance from 25 to 20 miles per week. Avoiding start-stop patterns of exercising is another factor in being able to maintain a healthy weight in the long term.

This brings us back to the importance of diet quality when you engage in regular exercise, irrespective of its intensity or duration. A scientific study from 2009, published under the provocative title, "Exercise alone is not enough: weight loss also needs a healthy diet," underscores our experience and observations in this regard.

A team of nutritionists and exercise physiologists wanted to understand why, in the majority of exercise intervention studies done up until that date, weight loss was so often reported as small and not long-lasting. They recruited 58 obese men and women and prescribed an exercise routine to burn about 500 calories per session, five times a week, at an intensity of 70% maximum heart rate. The study lasted for 12 weeks. Their body weight and various other health markers were assessed at weeks 5, 8, and 12.

Though the average reduction in body weight was significant---about seven pounds---there was a wide individual variation in the loss. As the scientists asked why, they found, in their words, "those participants who failed to lose meaningful weight increased their food intake and reduced their intake of fruits and vegetables." Their conclusion was clear: "a healthy diet is still required for weight loss to occur."

Failure to change unhealthy eating habits undermines the weight-supportive role of exercise. In a typical session of 30 minutes or so of exercise in a gym, you might burn 200 to 300 calories, but if you chase that down afterwards with an energy bar and a container of Gatorade, all of a sudden, the benefits of that exercise session have been virtually wiped out.

You cannot exercise away or outrun a bad diet and that is another reason why so many diet plans fail!

Williams P. Et al. "Asymmetric Weight Gain and Loss From Increasing and Decreasing Exercise." Medicine & Science in Sports and Exercise. 2008 February.
Caudwell P. Et al. "Exercise alone is not enough: weight loss also needs a healthy diet?" Public Health Nutrition. 2009 September.

What Happens to Fat Cells When You Lose Pounds?

Most health professionals and members of the public would fail if this question were a quiz: what happens to fat cells when you lose weight?

Do fat cells just magically disappear? Do they shrink first and then evaporate? Do the cells migrate into your digestive system and get expelled as body waste? Or, do the fat cells get converted to energy, which is the answer that most physicians might give.

Providing the right answer to this question gives us another glimpse into why the right healthy diet married to regular exercise is so integral to natural and sustainable weight loss.

Two scientists at the University of New South Wales, in Sydney, Australia - Ruben Meerman and Andrew Brown - give us this insight into the fat cell loss process. "Fat is converted to carbon dioxide, and water. You exhale the carbon dioxide and the water mixes into your circulation until it's lost as urine or sweat. If you lose 10 pounds of fat, precisely 8.4 pounds comes out through your lungs, and the remaining 1.6 pounds turns into water. In other words, nearly all the weight we lose is exhaled."

So, the regular exercise connection to diet and weight loss is now impossible to ignore. To accelerate losing weight, you must vaporize fat cells, which means you need to exercise to give yourself a process through which you can expel the fat cells through your lungs and sweat the rest of the fat cells out, as a byproduct of your physical exertions.

"Where fat goes when you lose weight." Ruben Meerman and Andrew Brown. CNN. March 26, 2018.

Combinations of Factors that Keep the Weight Off

We certainly don't want to leave you with the impression that successful long-term weight loss is unlikely or even unattainable. Since 1994, the National Weight Control Registry (NWCR) has kept detailed records on persons who have lost 30 or more pounds and maintained that loss for more than a year.

The idea behind the registry, which by 2019, had more than 10,000 people from all 50 states in it, was to document how they kept the weight off for up to five years and more. After surveying their experiences, scientists involved with the registry reported: "We found very little similarity in how these individuals lost weight but some common behaviors in how they are keeping their weight off."

Here are some of the attributes in common and most often identified among the successful long-term dieters in the database:

- Their most popular form of exercise was walking.

- They exercise about an hour a day.

- They eat breakfast every day.

- They eat a relatively low-fat diet.

- They weigh themselves with regularity.

- Most are self-described morning people.

Stankus T. "Reviews of Science for Science Librarians: The National Weight Control Registry—25 Years of Compiling Strategies Used by Long Term Weight Loss Maintainers." Reviews of Science for Science Librarians. 2019 April.

- They tend to watch less than 10 hours of television each week.

- Their motivation for keeping the weight off comes mostly from their recovery from a health scare, or from having a desire to live a longer life while staying healthy, rather than from a desire to be slimmer.

- They are more willing than most people to change their everyday behaviors and try new ways of living their lives until they find attitudes and behaviors that work best for them to accomplish their goals.

One more common denominator among people in the registry is that nearly all had failed several times to lose weight, but they kept experimenting to find an approach that worked for them in the long term. Sustaining weight loss isn't easy, though the registry proves that it's possible, and once it's achieved, the experience becomes truly life-changing in multiple positive ways.

Hill JO. Et al. "The National Weight Control Registry: Is it Useful in Helping Deal with Our Obesity Epidemic?" J Nutr Ed & Behav. 2005 August.

Highlights

OF PART TWO

Lifestyle decisions ultimately determine your health destiny, so to lose weight steadily and sustain that loss over time, you must build a mindset and a lifestyle for healthier habits.

Diet program adherence is a key factor in determining whether weight loss is sustainable in the long term.

Most popular diets fail to emphasize consuming essential nutrients that simultaneously provide nutrient density and quality in sufficient portions and combinations.

A raw food diet has demonstrated in scientific studies a consistent ability to shed more pounds and keep those pounds off in the long-term than other diets that have been studied.

Weight loss drugs are expensive and not always safe, and their long-term effectiveness in keeping the weight off remains questionable at best.

Some weight loss supplements have been found to be tainted with prescription drugs that call into question their purity and reliability.

Exercise must be regular and done the year round; otherwise, every time you quit exercising you will gain back some weight regardless of your diet.

Most popular diet programs have been found in scientific studies to be highly deficient in essential micronutrients that are necessary to sustain weight loss over time and protect against disease.

When you lose weight, the fat cells convert to carbon dioxide, and the water becomes sweat or urine; that makes exercise even more important in order to help flush out the fat cells.

Common behaviors that scientists have found to keep weight off for five years and more include walking an hour a day, eating breakfast every day, having a low-fat diet, weighing yourself regularly, watching less than 10 hours of television a week, and having a desire for a longer life.

PART THREE:

Proven Strategies for Self-Healing

Mind Strength for Weight Health

Food Choices for Weight Health

Body Tune-Ups for Weight Health

Lifestyle Rituals for Weight Health

Mind Strength for Weight Health

Train Your Brain to Resist Weight Gain

For you to initiate behavioral changes that will make long-term weight maintenance possible, it's often necessary to replace bad habits with new more positive habits. To accomplish that, you may need to learn for yourself how to transform bad habits rather than just trying to suppress them.

An effective change approach needs to stress the importance of having a clear direction, sufficient motivation, and a supportive environment to create a pattern for positive change to occur, according to a 2010 book, Switch: How to Change Things When Change Is Hard, by Chip Heath and Dan Heath. For it to be successful, it must involve setting behavioral goals using actionable steps that are small enough for occasional victories to be declared. Most normal people can't just declare, 'I will lose weight this year,' and then follow through and succeed; you must set weekly, even daily goals.

So instead of general or open-ended commitments such as 'I intend to exercise more,' set a specific daily goal, like: "I will work out on a bicycle for 20 minutes a day." It's important to put a practical plan in place that is clear, and you can follow through with. To illustrate, if you intend to eat more vegetables, have them already prepared and placed around your home, vehicle, and workplace, so they are readily available and remain a visual focus for you each day. As you accumulate these small wins, they establish milestones for reaching the bigger victories of achieving or maintaining weight loss.

To underscore this advice with support from scientific findings, British social scientists evaluated the results of 129 studies assessing the effectiveness of health behavior change strategies. It became clear from their analysis that sustainable behavioral change must come from positive thinking combined with the setting of self-motivated goals that are relatively small and specific and continuous.

Within the psychology field, a behavioral change approach with the most widespread acceptance and evidence for effectiveness is called the Transtheoretical model (TTM), which was first developed in the 1980s to treat alcohol addiction. This approach revolves around the 'stages of change,' in which a person seeking behavioral modification follows a five-stage progression: they go from precontemplation, to contemplation, then preparation, followed by taking action or maintenance of the behavioral change. A sixth stage in this model involves relapse since most everyone experiences some failures in their attempts at goal adherence, and the trick is to perceive the periodic fall downs as learning, not as failure.

Each stage of change becomes preparation for the next stage, and at each of these transition stages, different strategies come into play to sustain this behavioral change. The TTM model has been shown in experiments to be particularly effective in treating people who have issues with their diet and weight.

Financial incentives might also help to reinforce a weight loss state of mind. Willpower to break bad habits, such as overeating, or to reinforce good habits, such as sticking to weight loss goals, can be reinforced with the right combination of incentives, according to this 2023 study in the Journal of the American Medical Association.

Researchers randomized 1,280 adults, average age of 47 years, located in New York City and Los Angeles, into two inventive financial strategies to pursue weight management goals. Financial incentives of up to $750 were linked to weight loss over a period of six months. The financial incentives produced significant weight loss compared to a comparable control group of participants who received only educational support without such financial incentives.

There is evidence that even just one period of weight loss success instills the mental framework necessary for some people to achieve future weight loss success, despite any lapses that might have occurred in their self-discipline resulting in weight gain. Psychologists who have studied this phenomenon of dietary failure and success describe it as a goal conflict model of eating behavior, a friction between two seemingly incompatible goals---weight control and eating enjoyment.

In food-rich environments, dieters often fail in their weight control goals, but "there is a minority of restrained eaters," wrote the authors of a 2013 Psychological Review study, "for whom, most likely due to past success in exerting self-control, tasty high-calorie food has become associated with weight control thoughts. For them, exposure to palatable food increases the accessibility of the weight control goal, enabling them to control their body weight in food-rich environments."

If only we could use our thoughts alone to control our food choices. Unfortunately, what confronts us is somewhat more complex.

"Effectiveness of Goal-Directed and Outcome-Based Financial Incentives for Weight Loss in Primary Care Patients With Obesity Living in Socioeconomically Disadvantaged Neighborhoods: A Randomized Clinical Trial." Ladapo JA. Et al. JAMA Internal Medicine. 2023 January.
Fisher EB. Et al. "Behavior Matters." American Journal of Preventive Medicine. 2011.
Prochaska JO. Et al. "The Transtheoretical Model of Health Behavior Change." Am J Health Promotion. 1997 October.
Stroebe W. Et al. "Why most dieters fail but some succeed: a goal conflict model of eating behavior." Psychol Rev. 2013 January.

Does Your Stomach Control Your Food Choices?

"It's only human for us to think our brain controls our choices about which foods we will eat. But that appearance of choice may be an illusion, now that we know evidence exists showing how several species of bacteria living in our guts may determine how our stomachs override our brains."

Australian and Portuguese Neuroscientists made the discovery that two gut bacteria species, Acetobacter pomorum and Lactobacilli, collaborate and signal the brain to influence our dietary choices. These bacteria in our stomach and intestines act as predictors of missing key nutrients the body needs. These bacteria literally reprogram the body's nutrient priorities through some sort of chemical signaling exchange to alter appetite.

Previous studies of the gut have established a relationship between diseases like obesity and the gut's microbiome, a term referring to the environment within which these microorganisms live and influence our health destiny. This research underscores how important intestinal health is to our body weight, and how taking probiotic supplements may be something you need to add to your repertoire of fat-fighting techniques.

(To learn how to test your gut biome to assist your weight loss goals, go to our website: www.selfhealingdiet.com)

That old expression, 'your eyes are bigger than your stomach,' used to mean that you visualized the food you put on your plate as more appetizing than your hunger turns out to be. Now the expression has more validity based on scientific research showing how important visual cues are in triggering food cravings and uncontrolled eating.

To put the expression to the test, scientists did a study, appearing in the medical journal, *Obesity Research,* in which test subjects were blindfolded when they ate lunch. They consumed 22% less food and felt fuller faster than when they ate the same foods without blindfolds. Their eyes were indeed bigger than their stomachs.

In another study, conducted among 90 students in Germany, and published in the journal, *Food Quality and Preference*, eating without vision (visual cues) resulted in a 10% reduction in food consumption. Yet, significantly, study participants overestimated their food intake by 88% while blindfolded.

Goncalves R. Et al. "Commensal bacteria and essential amino acids control food choice behavior and reproduction." PLOS Biology. 2017 April. Linne Y. "Vision and eating behavior." Obesity Research. 2002 February.
Renner B. Et al. "Eating in the dark: A dissociation between perceived and actual food consumption." Food Quality and Preference. 2016 June.

This could provide a clue about the harsh bright lighting so often used in fast food restaurants, which seems to stimulate a greater perceived appetite in diners and resulting overconsumption. It may well be, based on these study results, the best dining ambiance to reduce overeating is in dimly lit settings, even candlelight. **Less visual stimulation can help you to reduce your calorie intake, promote more self-disciplined eating, help to encourage weight loss, and turn your dining experiences into more of a ritual and less of a monotonous habit.**

Learn to Delay Gratification

Anywhere between 40% and 97% of all people report experiencing food cravings, a desire to consume specific, usually unhealthy foods, according to survey results published in the science journal, *Appetite*. These cravings often lead to overeating, snacking and binge eating episodes that result in unhealthy weight gain.

Some people seem to be born with the ability to delay gratification and resist temptation, at least in the short term. A fascinating experiment from the 1960s makes this point. Social scientists examined self-control in 60 preschoolers by giving them a test: each child was placed in a small room with a marshmallow sitting on a table, and the child was told they could eat the marshmallow now, or if they waited for 15 minutes, they would be given two marshmallows.

Some children were able to wait for 15 minutes, while others struggled with the temptation and finally gave in and ate the marshmallow before their time was up. The children who were able to wait distracted themselves from yielding to temptation by covering their eyes or turning around to face the wall.

Four decades after this experiment, researchers tracked down 59 out of 60 of these children again (all of them are in their 40s) to find out how their self-control worked out in adulthood. Those kids who exercised self-control in the marshmallow test were still able to resist temptation as adults, whereas those who had failed as kids mostly continued to fail as adults, triggering problems with weight and substance abuse. These results were confirmed in brain scans that showed the temptation delayers had more activity in a region of their prefrontal cortex associated with impulse control than did those who yielded to temptation.

Lacaille J. Et al. "The effects of three mindfulness skills on chocolate cravings." Appetite. 2014 February.

> "It's important to point out, however, whether you were born with heightened self-control or not, you can still learn to develop that ability, or further enhance your capacity, by using the scientifically proven techniques we reveal in this book. You can literally train your brain to resist temptations and stick to a diet and exercise plan."

To resist the daily food temptations and resulting cravings that everyone encounters in the sensory-rich environment of our culture, any of which could contribute to the derailment of a weight maintenance plan, exercising self-discipline may require drawing upon 'skillpower,' a range of scientifically proven techniques that can assist in you remaining loyal to your dietary and exercise goals in order to keep excess weight off and enhance your quality of life.

We offer here a series of simple, portable and inexpensive techniques, all science tested, to manage your food consumption habits and cravings.

Casey BJ. Et al. "Behavioral and neural correlates of delay of gratification 40 years later." Proc Natl Acad Sciences. 2011 August.

Distract Yourself from Cravings

Distraction is an effective technique that magicians use to divert an audience's attention from how a trick is being performed. Study findings indicate that the same principle can be used, a form of mental sleight of hand, to loosen the hold of a food craving. Called 'mental resource blocking' by psychologists, it involves a variety of techniques to diminish food cravings, particularly among people sensitive to visual food cues.

Dutch brain researchers tested groups of people for their sensitivity to food images as they worked a puzzle to distract themselves from cravings. The 91 volunteers were assigned to a distraction group, or a control group. The distraction group engaged in a puzzle game for three minutes, rotating blocks of various shapes, which required them to use their visuospatial working memory. The control group viewed a blank computer screen for three minutes. Both groups were then allowed to eat unhealthy high calorie foods.

The distraction group participants recorded little or no cravings for the junk foods, while the control group displayed various levels of cravings for those high-calorie foods. This same team of scientists did a second study of 63 men and women who hadn't eaten to keep their hunger levels higher than normal. Those in the distraction group did a mental task using a code to convert numbers into letters, spelling a word, or erasing certain letters in a letter grid. As a reward at the conclusion of the study, participants were offered either a gift pen, or a piece of chocolate. Those in the distraction group, no matter how sensitive to food cues, were more likely to choose a pen rather than the chocolate, whereas those who had not done the distraction exercise were much more likely to select the chocolate.

By distracting yourself with a mental game or puzzle, even if it's a phone app version, you can neutralize cravings that might otherwise overwhelm you. By loading your brain with tasks while exposed to food temptations, your attention is distracted long enough to give you an opportunity to exercise self-control.

An alternative to self-distraction to manage food intake is to engage in a mindfulness practice while eating. To illustrate why this could be a difference maker for you, a 2022 study from The Netherlands surveyed the eating habits of 1,011 Dutch adults and found that the most common eating distractions were talking to others (32.7% of respondents) and watching television while eating (21.7% of those surveyed.) Only 18% of the people reported not having distractions during their meal times. It shouldn't come as any surprise that the scientists in this study found higher body mass index scores for the distracted eaters.

Add to self-distraction and mindfulness another tool developed by the field of positive psychology—acceptance.

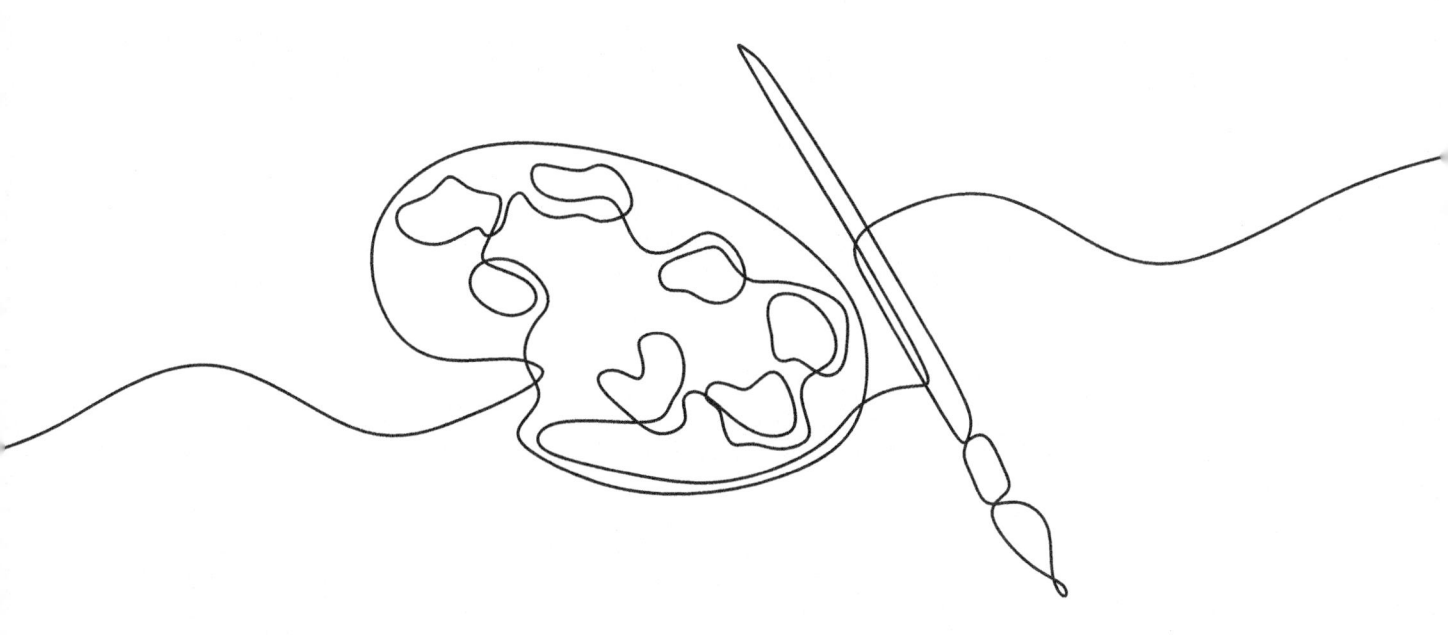

Van Dillen LF. Andrade J. "Derailing the streetcar named desire. Cognitive distractions reduce individual differences in cravings and unhealthy snacking in response to palatable food." Appetite. 2016 January. Also, Van Dillen LF. Et al. "Turning a blind eye to temptation: how cognitive load can facilitate self-regulation." J Pers Soc Psychol. 2013 March.
Floor van Meer, Et al. "Daily distracted consumption patterns and their relationship with BMI." Appetite. 2022 September.

Try Acceptance, Not Suppression

Some research findings indicate that you can control a food craving more readily by accepting it, than by trying to suppress it.

In one study of 48 overweight women, each was assigned to one of two groups - an acceptance of cravings group or a distraction intervention group who simply tried mental strategies of distraction from cravings. Each group carried around a box of candy for 72 hours, trying to abstain from consuming any. Using the acceptance-based coping strategies resulted in lower cravings and reduced consumption.

A second study, with 98 undergraduate students, involved them carrying around transparent boxes of chocolate Hershey's Kisses for 48 hours. They had been instructed not to eat any of the candies. The students were divided into a no-intervention group, a control-based group that used distraction, and an acceptance group. Based on measures of cravings and consumption, the acceptance group exercised the most ability to control cravings.

In practice, this means when a craving arises, stop what you are doing and say to yourself, "I notice the craving; I accept there is a craving in my body and mind." Next, say to yourself, "I recognize that I am not my craving. My craving does not define who I am."

Next, say to yourself: "I see how this craving is temporary. It will pass. I choose not to act on this craving."

By accepting food cravings as a natural part of being human, this helps to eliminate the shame that comes from attempting to suppress a craving, but failing to do so. This 'self-surrender' helps to bring about self-compassion in order to diminish the power cravings exercise over you.

Forman EM. Et al. "Comparison of acceptance-based and standard cognitive-based coping strategies for craving sweets in overweight and obese women." Eating Behavior. 2013 January. Also, Forman EM. Et al. "A comparison of acceptance- and control-based strategies for coping with food cravings: an analog study." Behavior Research Therapy. 2007 October.

'Surf' Your Urges

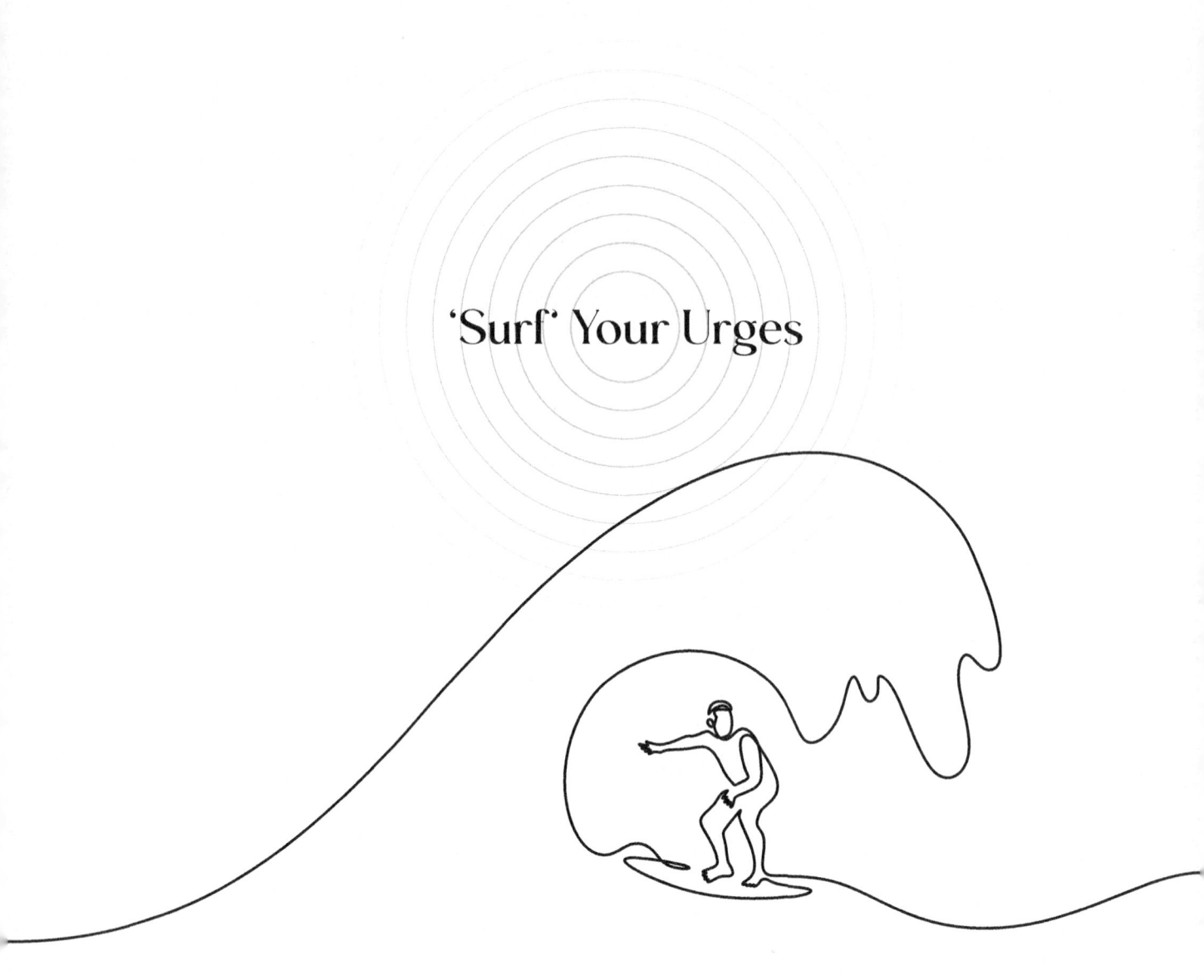

A Professor of Psychology at the University of Washington, Alan Marlatt, did a series of studies looking at controlling impulses revolving around substance abuse and ended up discovering something he called 'urge surfing,' a mindfulness technique to help resist urges such as cravings for unhealthy foods.

He concluded that trying to resist cravings is like standing under a waterfall - you get inundated. His research indicated that most cravings never last more than 30 minutes, so the trick is how to 'surf' them for that period of time without being swept up in them.

That's where the mindfulness meditation technique of urge surfing comes in. He tested the idea out on a group of 123 college students who wanted to resist their urges to smoke cigarettes. They were divided up into two groups: one that received mindfulness instructions, and a no-instruction control group. At the end of the study period, both groups had experienced similar measures of their urges to smoke, but the mindfulness group actually smoked far fewer cigarettes. Their response to their urges had been altered sufficiently to help them stay on the path toward smoking cessation.

How does this mindfulness practice help make the brain more immune to temptations? Professor Marlatt's scanning technology research into the brain regions involved with cravings discovered that mindfulness and its focus of attention actually disconnected, almost quite literally, the brain regions of the cravings network from each other, as if a short circuit had been introduced into an electrical system.

Subsequent scientific research affirmed Marlatt's findings. For example, the journal, *Frontiers of Psychology* reported in 2018 how "mindfulness training that targets reward- based learning may constitute an appropriate intervention to rewire the learning process around eating."

Or consider this conclusion in the science journal, *Current Obesity Reports*: "This review demonstrates strong support for the inclusion of mindful eating as a component of weight management programs and may provide substantial benefit to the treatment of overweight and obesity."

Additionally, in this 2017 study in which 46 adults went through a 6-month standard weight loss program or a mindfulness meditation program, those in the mindfulness group lost almost six pounds more than the standard group, through greater improvements in eating behaviors and dietary restraint, prompting the researchers to urge that the low-cost, portable mindfulness skill becomes a standard practice to use with overweight and obese adults.

Engaging in a quiet and still mindfulness practice has received widespread scientific support for its effectiveness in cravings control.

Bowen S. Marlatt A. "Surfing the urge: brief mindfulness-based intervention for college student smokers." Psychol Addict Behav. 2009 December.
Brewer JA. Et al. "Can Mindfulness Address Maladaptive Eating Behaviors? Why Traditional Diet Plans Fail and How New Mechanistic Insights May Lead to Novel Interventions." Front Psychol. 2018 September.
Dunn C. Et al. "Mindfulness Approaches and Weight Loss, Weight Maintenance, and Weight Regain." Curr Obes Rep. 2018 March.
Spadaro KC. Et al. "Effect of mindfulness meditation on short-term weight loss and eating behaviors in overweight and obese adults: A randomized controlled trial." J Complement Integr Med. 2017 December.

Researchers at Canada's McGill University had 196 volunteers to do one of three mindfulness practices to test their control over chocolate cravings. They either: 1) developed their awareness by taking notice of their thoughts; 2) accepted their thoughts without passing judgment on them; 3) or engaged in disidentification, or non-attachment, which is to think of the cravings as thoughts that are separate and apart from you.

All participants had reported having frequent and strong cravings for chocolate. After two weeks of mindfulness training, each participant was given a piece of chocolate to unwrap and touch for one minute. Then they rated how much they still craved the candy. The best results were achieved by the disidentification group, who "developed less-intense cravings for chocolate because they now perceived it as generally less desirable."

This disidentification technique resembles 'urge surfing,' created by the late psychologist, Alan Marlatt.

Lacaille J., et al. "The effects of three mindfulness skills on chocolate cravings." Appetite. 2014 February.

The Biggest Craving of All Is Chocolate

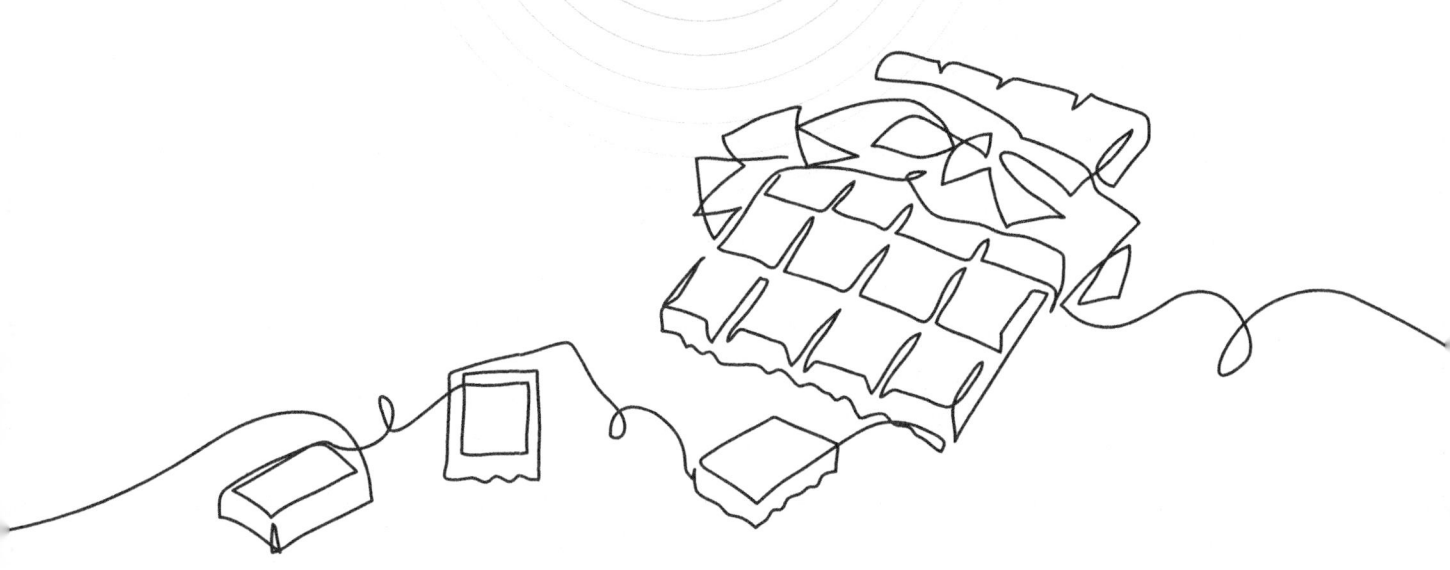

For many people, a craving for chocolate can be more powerful of an urge to contend with than any craving for something salty like potato chips, or craving anything fatty like pizza. Chocolate is a seductress like no other!

Among women, about half crave chocolate most acutely around the onset of menstruation. Once these women are in the postmenopausal phase of their life, chocolate cravings decrease only minimally (13% of women), so for many women the urge to consume it becomes a lifelong obsession.

Strengthening your willpower to neutralize your desire for chocolate can be as simple as walking away from it. Science evidence reveals that a brisk walk can make just about anyone forget the temptation that chocolate arouses.

Hormes JM. "Perimenstrual chocolate craving: What happens after menopause?" Appetite. 2009 October.

British and Austrian scientists placed 47 overweight persons, all obsessed with sugary snacks, through three days of chocolate abstinence by having one group do nothing special to combat chocolate cravings while the second group took a brisk 15-minute walk every time a chocolate urge was felt.

Whereas both groups engaged in several tasks to measure how distracting their cravings had become, it was the brisk walker group that greatly reduced their urge for chocolate. The walking ritual had made them more able to control their reactions to stress and food cues that normally would result in caving into their chocolate urges. Other research appearing in the journal, *Appetite,* uncovered similar results. Brisk 15-minute walks turned off the chocolate urges even after three days of abstaining from eating the substance.

The explanation offered by researchers explaining why fast walking distracts a person from cravings is that physical exertion helps to change moods and behaviors by altering the brain's blood chemistry to release hormones that act as counterweights to the sensation of cravings.

A contrasting approach to chocolate cravings, discussed earlier, published in the science journal, *Appetite,* and featured mindfulness skill practices tested on 196 subjects (three-fourths of them women) who had intense cravings for chocolate and a motivation to reduce those cravings. Half of the participants received two weeks of mindfulness awareness training, learning how to engage in disidentification when they felt cravings, while the other half did not receive this instruction.

As part of the disidentification training, participants were taught to use this thought process when they would crave chocolate: they would repeat these disidentifying statements -

---

Ledochowski L. Et al. "Acute effects of brisk walking on sugary snack cravings in overweight people, affect and responses to a manipulated stress situation and to a sugary snack cue: a crossover study." PLoS One. 2015. Also, Oh H. Et al. "A brisk walk, compared with being sedentary, reduces attentional bias and chocolate cravings among regular chocolate eaters with different body mass." Appetite. 2013. Also, Taylor AH. Et al. "Acute effects of brisk walking on urges to eat chocolate, affect, and responses to a stressor and chocolate cue. An experimental study." Appetite. 2009.

> "I perceive myself as separate from my thoughts and feelings about the chocolate that I crave"... "I do not identify with my thoughts about the craving"... "I see the cravings as just a thought that I am having in my mind"... "I can observe feelings about my cravings without being drawn into them"... "I view my thoughts and feelings about the craving from a wider perspective".

As the science team concluded from their findings, the mindfulness skills were "successful at teaching disidentification, which led to greater reductions in chocolate cravings and a smaller increase in cravings when exposed to chocolate," compared to the control group. Furthermore, "disidentification can be taught in a relatively short timeframe and is thus an ideal candidate as a strategy that can be included in real-world interventions designed to help people better manage their food obsessions."

Lacaille J. Et al. "The effects of three mindfulness skills on chocolate cravings." Appetite. 2014 May.

'Tap Away' Cravings

Based on the principles of acupuncture, a clinical psychologist created a system of finger tapping on 'meridian points' of the human body to help strengthen willpower in the face of temptations.

It's called the Emotional Freedom Technique (EFT), and its effectiveness has been tested in several medical studies. Australian scientists, for instance, put 96 overweight or obese adults through four weeks of EFT training and then assessed their progress at 6 and 12-month intervals. At the study's end, the researchers concluded: "Significant improvements occurred in weight, body mass index, food cravings, subjective power of food craving restraint, and psychological coping."

Neuroimaging of the brains of people engaged in tapping away cravings found that the finger tapping decreased arousal in a part of the brain usually stimulated by stress or negative emotions. That decreased stimulation assisted in deactivating the impact of food cravings. To learn the steps on how to use the tapping technique, please go to our website, theselfhealingdiet.com.

Stapleton P. Et al. "A randomized clinical trial of a meridian-based intervention for food cravings with six-month follow-up." Behaviour Change. 2011.

Mental Imagery & Sounds Can Assist You

When people feel cravings urges, they often experience vivid imagery of the foods they desire, triggering memories of how good the food tastes and smells and the pleasant sensations associated with eating it. Psychologists writing in the science journal, *Frontiers in Psychiatry,* examined the study research surrounding the use of mental imagery to reduce food cravings and found compelling evidence that anyone can learn to summon competing images to counteract mental images of tempting foods. By performing a visual task, such as using a cell phone screen to project a flickering pattern, the vividness of imagined foods is diminished, and the cravings reduced.

Chocolate cravings, in particular, have been shown in studies to be affected by visualizing focusing on the image of a bright and colorful rainbow. "It is important to note," wrote the researchers, "that people need not be good visualizers, in general, to derive benefit from imagery-based carving reduction tasks, thus demonstrating applicability across the board."

Some studies produced findings that when participants imagined themselves in their favorite settings doing their favorite activities, not only was the intensity of the good cravings reduced, their actual daily food intake was lowered. These effects can be produced by mobile apps that prompt users to imagine a specific scene as soon as they experience food cravings.

Though many guided imagery interventions produce effects that don't last long beyond their use in the moment, evidence is consistent these techniques do maintain their beneficial effects over time, over weeks and months, with repeated use, making them effective for in-the-moment-restraint.

Repetition of an inspiring phrase or slogan that encompasses your goal, such as, "Not eating this food will help make me the person I want to be," can help you to resist temptation and resultant cravings when you are exposed to unhealthy foods.

In a series of studies with people who had nicotine cravings, scientists at Columbia University and Yale University School of Medicine taught test participants to think about all of the consequences of smoking cigarettes every time they felt a nicotine urge. That thought process helped them regulate the neural pathways in their brain triggered by those cravings.

These results were affirmed in other researchers in Holland, who used functional magnetic resonance imaging of the brain of test subjects, to document how thinking of the health consequences of eating something unhealthy and fattening decreases activity in brain regions connected to food cravings.

If you make lists of all the reasons you shouldn't yield to temptation and consume unhealthy, fattening foods, you can either memorize the slogans you create, or write them down for future reference. Recite your list mentally or out loud when you confront a craving. You can even add a visualization to the affirmation by imagining how much better you will look and feel if you resist the urges. You will be training your brain to lessen the influence of those brain regions influenced by cravings cues.

Kemps E. Tiggemann M. "A Role for Mental Imagery in the Experience and Reduction of Food Cravings." Front Psychiatry. 2014 November.
Kober H. Et al. "Regulation of craving by cognitive strategies in cigarette smokers." Drug & Alcohol Dependence. 2010 January.
Siep N. Et al. "Fighting food temptations: the modulating effects of short-term cognitive reappraisal, suppression and up-regulation on mesocorticolimbic activity related to appetitive motivation." Neuroimage. 2012 March.

Visualization to Focus Your Mind

Your mind and the power of your imagination can be indispensable tools to help trigger physiological changes. Doing visualization exercises, otherwise known as mental imagery, is one of the elements of our own Hippocrates Wellness weight loss program synergy.

We had an incredibly obese woman here at Hippocrates, for example, who put her face as cutouts on photographs of young models, and then she posted them on the walls of her home. It gave her a constant source of inspiration. She created a visual image of who she wanted to be as the first concrete step in making that her reality. Every time she wanted to eat, she looked at those images. She ended up losing about 250 pounds using this approach.

These sorts of profound 'mind-over-matter' transformations, based on accessing imagination and believing in its power, are becoming more common as people commit to using visualization. As an illustration, there was a British woman who lost 56 pounds after having five sessions with a hypnotist, who had convinced her to believe that she had undergone gastric stomach band surgery, shrinking her stomach to the size of a golf ball.

These hypnotic sessions implanting a visual memory of an imaginary surgery were so vivid that 35-year-old Marion Corns told the news media, "Bizarrely, I can remember the clink of the surgeon's knife and the smell of anesthetic." She no longer had much of an appetite, and she began to lose about three pounds a week.

"I had tried every other diet and exercise plan the world has to offer," she said. "I've tried tablets, WeightWatchers, Atkins, Slimfast, milkshakes and even a personal trainer, but none of them helped me. Now I am able to shed up to three pounds a week because I believe I have had a band fitted into my stomach." That strong belief stopped her binge eating, and she began to drop the excess weight.

To test how far our beliefs can take us, when it comes to fitness, the housekeeping staff of a major hotel was told by Harvard University researchers that the exercise they got every day, just from cleaning hotel rooms, had given them a heightened state of fitness. A month later, the researchers found that these housekeepers had lost weight and reduced their body mass index without doing anything other than their normal routine. Their belief about being fit and the image of themselves that gave them, had set in motion measurable changes in their body composition.

Mental rehearsal has been a form of visualization used for several decades by athletes before engaging in competitions. It involves the mental preparation of visualizing the successful completion of the physical act. You have a specific goal in mind; you imagine the scene with as much detail as you can summon, including the emotions you are feeling about your success, you snap a mental photograph of yourself standing in triumph, and then you practice creating and holding this imagery before the actual event.

Champion golfer Jack Nicklaus often declared "I never hit a shot, not even in practice, without having a very sharp in-focus picture of it in my head." Many other athletes have admitted to employing the same technique for success.

Exercise psychologists did experiments that revealed that thoughts produce the same instructions to the body as the initiation of actions, with mental imagery affecting such brain processes as motor control, attention, perception and executive functions of planning. At the same time, this sort of mental practice enhances confidence and motivation.

Exercise experts writing in the *Journal of Sports Science Medicine,* revealed in 2016, how they reviewed the scientific literature on the use of mental imagery {visualizing internally rather than looking at external images} to build muscle strength and found "advantageous effects of internal imagery (range from 2.6 to 136.3%) for strength performance."

"I'm on the hypno-diet: Wife loses four stone after therapist convinces her she's got a gastric band." Eleanor Glover. The Daily Mail (UK). May 21, 2009.
Archer S. "Belief in exercise improves results." IDEA Fitness Journal. 2007.
Slimani M. Et al. "Effects of Mental Imagery on Muscular Strength in Healthy and Patient Participants: A Systematic Review." J Sports Sci Med. 2016 August.

One of the studies reviewed used 30 volunteers who either performed 'mental contractions of a little finger or did actual finger exercises. This test lasted 12 weeks, at 15 minutes a day, five days a week. At the end of the experiment, the mental group had increased their finger strength by 35%, compared to 53% for the group who actually did the physical exercises of the finger. This experiment provided, needless to say, significant proof of how powerful the human mind can be when it relies on imagery to improve the body.

If visualization and mental imagery work on building muscle, why couldn't the same 'mind over matter' concept work with weight loss? There is direct scientific evidence that indeed it can!

Perhaps the most convincing evidence for the power of imagery to affect weight was produced in 2019 by British scientists, who recruited 141 overweight or obese adults and divided them up into two groups: one received sessions of motivational interviewing, the other group got visualization sessions called Functional Imagery Training. Each group started the clinical trial by receiving two sessions of an hour each, followed every two weeks by 'booster calls' of 15 minutes. Physical and body composition assessments of all participants were made at six months and twelve months.

At six months, mental imagery participants had lost an average of eight pounds and seven centimeters of waist circumference, compared to negligible losses by the motivational interview group. At twelve months, mental imaging group members had lost more than 12 pounds and nine centimeters of waist circumference, while the motivation group had shed less than one pound of weight. As the research team wrote, when their study was published in the *International Journal of Obesity,* mental imagery provided "substantial benefits for weight loss and maintenance of weight reduction."

There you have it! Engaging in a daily, long-term ritual of visualizing yourself at the weight you ideally want to be, can be an important tool to help you achieve your goal.

Ranganathan VK. Et al. "From mental power to muscle power—gaining strength by using the mind." Neuropsychologia. 2004.
Solbrig L. Et al. "Functional imagery training versus motivational interviewing for weight loss: a randomized controlled trial of brief individual interventions for overweight and obesity." Int J Obes. 2019 April.

Use Mind Relaxation for Weight Loss

To change long-term unhealthy behaviors and facilitate lasting weight loss, some health coaches are turning their clients on to the benefits of mindfulness and meditation to help reprogram their subconscious mind, rewiring those parts of the brain that weaponize toxic food habits. Not only can a meditative practice help to strengthen the immune system and remove subconscious barriers, such as food issues from childhood, that sabotage the cultivation of a weight loss state of mind, an inner practice can instill positive attitudes that promote a healthier relationship to food and even engender compassion for yourself when you fail to reach your goals.

Mindfulness and meditation can be combined into one practice, or can be undertaken separately as part of your weight loss plan. While the two practices can overlap and support each other, there are subtle differences. Mindfulness is a careful and heightened awareness, a state of being in which you pay close attention to everything around you, as well as your feelings and thoughts and movements. Meditation, by contrast, involves a seated, eyes-closed, slow and deep breathing practice, done in a quiet place, to clear the mind of all extraneous thoughts. There are many types or styles of meditation, such as a focus on breath awareness, visualization, affirmations, and feelings of loving-kindness. Research these various types and choose the practice that feels best suited to you.

Science research affirms in various ways the effective role that meditation and mindfulness can play in pursuing sustained weight loss. In a 2017 review contrasting the results of 19 studies, the science journal *Obesity Reviews* found the two practices "largely effective in reducing obesity-related eating behaviors," with an average weight loss of 6.8 to 7.5 pounds reported over a period

"Here's How Meditation Helps With Weight Loss." Dina Kaplan. Forbes. January 28, 2018.

of weeks. The weight loss results varied, as you can imagine, based on each person's level of commitment to the practice.

A more recent evaluation (2021) in the science journal, *Appetite,* compared the results of 12 randomized controlled trials of mindfulness-based interventions for weight loss, including binge eating. Though there was variability in the durations of these study interventions, the shorter interventions of 6 weeks duration with a mindfulness meditation practice produced noteworthy reductions in average body mass comparable to the 2017 study review just mentioned.

We can say with confidence that as a support system for making positive changes in your life around food and eating, meditation and mindfulness can inspire you to evolve healthier habits—and steady and sustainable weight loss--- if you engage with the practices in a spirit of commitment, patience, and compassion for yourself.

"Mindfulness-based interventions for weight loss: a systematic review and meta-analysis." Carriere K. Et al. Obesity Reviews. october 2017.
"The outcomes of mindfulness-based interventions for Obesity and Binge Eating Disorder: A meta-analysis of randomized controlled trials." Mercado D. Et al. Appetite. 2021 November. Also, "Does Meditation Help You Lose Weight?" WebMD. August 1, 2014. https://www.webmd.com/balance/features/meditation-hypertension-and-weight-loss

Experiment with Behavioral Change Technology

Breaking bad habits and embracing healthier ways of being, to advance your weight maintenance goals, may necessitate some experimentation with behavioral change technologies that are now widely available. These devices assist users in staying on target by adhering to steps and schedules.

Over the past decade, there has been an explosion in the number of technological gadgets designed to facilitate the breaking of bad habits, while instilling healthy behaviors. 'Mobile Health' is the general term for using mobile phones and other wireless technology. It involves the measuring, monitoring, and educating of patients about their health risk factors, and their progress in reaching health goals, such as losing weight, exercising more frequently, and eating a healthier diet.

Among the gadget categories are the wearable monitor apps that you actually attach to yourself. Then there are the reportable apps (they send you messages and reminders), including smartphones, connected monitors, electronic health records, diet journaling apps, and fitness apps.

All of these various gadgets are intended to motivate users to initiate action for better health, to stick with their program of action, and to do so until an old habit is broken and a new, healthier behavior has taken firm root. Make sure to attach an EMF protection product like our HHI 360 for your technological equipment and our HHI Pulse for yourself. See our website for more details. www.hippocrateswellness.org

Many of the software products track ideas from B.J. Fogg, head of the Persuasive Technology Lab at Stanford University. He created a three-step process for the design of behavioral change technologies:

1) *Be Specific,* identify the target outcomes and goals.

2) *Make It Easy,* set up the new behavior desired, so it's simple and easy to accomplish.

3) *Trigger Behavior,* create prompts that keep the desired behavior in focus.

You may wonder how effective these various devices are in triggering, and helping to sustain, healthy changes in behavior. Creating rewards is one of the most important keys to sustainable behavioral changes, and these can be external rewards, in the form of money and prizes. Although, it is important that any incentive or reward program also instills in the user a feeling of pride and achievement.

A 2015 survey of 10 studies that assessed the effectiveness of mobile apps measuring physical activity, in which the app owners self-reported their exercise progress, generally found "significant increases" in physical activity. This seemed to suggest the measuring of progress helped to instill pride of achievement.

In the *American Journal of Health Education,* researchers described a 12-week intervention they did with 40 test subjects, average age of 32 years, 85% of whom were women. The intervention used Exergame smartphone applications with motivational messaging to test whether physical activity could be increased. Results were positive that Exergame kept physical exertion high, compared to the control group.

Findings from another 10 studies targeting weight loss were also analyzed by the researchers writing in the journal, JMIR mHealth, and uHealth. For these smartphone interventions, most of the studies reported either higher amounts of weight loss from the smartphone apps and their prompts or lower body mass index readings as a result of using the technologies.

Study participants generally preferred apps that were fast and easy to use. Also important to most users was the ability of wearable and phone apps to raise their awareness of certain behaviors, while providing cues to take action. They enjoyed having the ability to monitor their progress over

Patel MS. "Wearable Devices as Facilitators, Not Drivers, of Health Behavior Change." Journal of the American Medical Association. January 8, 2015.
Cowdery J. Et al. "Exergame Apps and Physical Activity: The Results of the ZOMBIE Trial." American Journal of Health Education. 2015.
Payne HE. Et al. "Behavioral Functionality of Mobile Apps in Health Interventions: A Systematic Review of the Literature." JMIR mHealth. February 26, 2015.

time using measures of long-term health outcomes as a result of the app coaching, though some users also reported they became irritated by apps that issued repeated prompts. Another important attribute was the social support afforded by apps that link users together, so people are able to offer each other encouragement and advice.

Action Tip: Breathwalk Away From Cravings

For some people, food cravings relief could be as easy as taking a few deep breaths and going for a short walk.

Breathwalking is a practice and tradition rooted in Zen Buddhism. It uses the development of a more peaceful and contented mind to better control physical sensations, especially food cravings. Doing this practice involves synchronizing footsteps with breathing, a sort of walking meditation. This can be of particular benefit to those who can't or won't sit still in one place, meditating for any period of time.

Practitioners walk around a room clockwise; one hand closed in a fist with the other hand covering it. With each step, they take a full breath and release it with the next step. Your walking pace can be slow or faster, so long as your breath and step remains synchronized.

Scientists from Harvard Medical School did a study of breathwalking for the *World Journal of Gastroenterology*, using 17 persons who were overweight or obese. Their body composition was measured and blood samples taken, before and after one-hour sessions of breathwalking. The study volunteers breath walked three times a week for six months.

At three months and six months, results were measured. Nearly all of the participants experienced dramatic improvements in all measures of mood states. When the experiment began, half of the study participants expressed negative mood states, such as fear, anguish, anger and depression. After six months, only 6% of them felt negativity.

Negative moods are a known trigger for food cravings (sugar in particular) and emotional eating. By elevating moods, breathwalking turned out to be a therapeutic remedy for controlling cravings.

Here is how to do it.

Do 10 minutes of warm-up, moving your arms and legs while doing conscious deep breathing, by inflating your stomach with air, and slowly exhaling it.

Five minutes is then spent mentally sensing your body posture while walking with conscious awareness to synchronize your breathing. The next 25 minutes are spent walking quicker, inhaling and exhaling, accompanied by mentally repeating such positive reinforcement phrases as: "I feel no desire for toxic foods."

Spend the final few minutes doing standing stretches. As you do this, feel yourself in control of your thoughts and your actions.

For those of you wanting technological support for this practice, a walking-aware mobile app was recently created and designed to help synchronize breathing and walking.

What makes Breathwalking effective, according to the study researchers, is that walking stimulates your circulatory system to release hormones and elevate your mood, while the synchronized breathing calms your metabolism, stabilizes your heart rate, and releases serotonin, the 'feel good' hormone.

Vazquez-Vandyck M. Et al. "Effect of Breathwalk on body composition, metabolic and mood state in chronic hepatitis C patients with insulin resistance syndrome." World Journal of Gastroenterology. 2007 December.
Also, Gurgevich S. Nicolai JP. "Obesity and the Stress Connection: Mind-Body Therapies for Weight Control." Integrative Weight Management. 2014 March. Also, Bhajan Y. Singh-Khalsa G. Breathwalk: Breathing Your Way to a Revitalized Body, Mind and Spirit. Random House, New York. 2000. Also, Meng-Chieh Y."Multimedia-Assisted Breathwalk Aware System." Biomedical Engineering Transactions. 2012 July.

Action Tip: Dissolve Your Toxic Urges

To surf an urge, Professor Alan Marlatt recommends that as soon as you feel a craving you want to dissolve, sit down with your back supported in a chair. Close your eyes and begin to focus on your breathing, the slow and steady in and out of your breath.

As you focus on your breath, make a mental note of the desire you feel and notice the related thoughts that arise around it. Feel into the urge and where it comes up in your body.

As thoughts continue to arise, say to yourself, these are just thoughts, and I don't have to act on them. Don't dwell on these thoughts. Just let them slip by one by one, as if you are watching leaves in a creek float by.

Keep gently bringing your attention back to your breath.

Keep this focus on your breathing going for as long as you can. You will find your thoughts begin to shift away from the urge to consume something. You are diminishing the power of the urges by distracting yourself from them rather than trying to summon willpower to resist them.

Continue riding out these urges until they go away. Over time, this practice will come more naturally to you.

Action Tip: Distance Yourself from the Craving

Mindfulness-Based Relapse Prevention involves bringing mindful awareness to cravings by creating mind 'space' between you and the craving you feel. You simply pause and observe the present moment, taking note of cravings and associated feelings, so you can begin to break the pattern of automatically reacting to the sensations of cravings.

To start, sit quietly and close your eyes.

Next, feel into those areas of your body where you most sense your cravings originate from. It could be your stomach, your head, or your mouth. Then focus your attention on that area of the body.

As you focus with your imagination, ask yourself some questions. What does my sensation feel like? What does that area really look like? What would the craving look like if I could picture it outside of my body?

With these questions, you mentally separate yourself from the craving.

By distancing yourself from your chocolate craving, with practice, you come to realize that you are not your thoughts. That helps make chocolate less desirable.

As you do this practice over time, you train your brain to rewire itself, so your cravings lose their strength. Positive thoughts and habits begin to take their place and you no longer automatically react on impulses and cravings.

You now have a greater capacity to stop yourself in the moment, knowing that you can make a choice to travel in a different direction and at different speeds.

Marlatt A. Bowen S. "Surfing the urge: brief mindfulness-based intervention for college student smokers." Psychological Addictive Behavior. 2009 December.

Action Tip: Visualize Your Weight Goals

To experiment with mental imagery to support your weight loss goals, please go to www.theselfhealingdiet.com where you can find an exercise that feels right for you. It should be an exercise that proves effective at programming your subconscious mind with positive reinforcement.

Also, you can use the following visualization exercise or a variation, whatever your personal needs. As preparation to begin, create the image of yourself that you want to achieve. It might be using a photograph of yourself at an age when you were at the weight that you currently desire to be at again. It might be an image of someone whose weight you admire. The image should represent an achievable goal for you, not a fantasy of you as a SuperHero or having a world-class beach body.

Next, find a quiet place, as you would in a meditation, where you won't be disturbed by other people, animals, or by cell phones, and other noisy distractions. It can be in your home, or it can be somewhere in nature. Make this spot your daily retreat space.

To start, have the image you aspire to emulate firmly fixed in your mind's eye as if it were a post it-note behind your eyelids. Now close your eyes, keeping the image as focused as you are able.

Take a slow deep breath in, hold it for a couple of seconds, then release it with a slow breath out Continue with this breathing rhythm while keeping your attention on the image.

If errant thoughts arise, don't focus on them, simply let them slip by without mental commentary. If the image you are focused on begins to blur and become indistinct, use your will to bring it back into focus, as you would sharpen your eyesight on a faraway object.

Keep your breath rhythm going, and keep refocusing on the image. Feel yourself slipping deeper into relaxation.

At this point, you can add an affirmation, if you like. Repeat it to yourself silently.

For instance, "This is the person I desire to be. This is the person I WILL become."

Repeat your affirmation over and over as you keep your breath slow and easy and your attention remains focused on the image in your mind's eye.

Do this visualization routine for 10 minutes every day, or if you can spare the time, do it twice a day, in the morning and evening.

Food Choices for Weight Health

Distracted Eating Invites Obesity

How much food we eat at any given meal gets influenced by factors we don't normally consider when thinking about our dining rituals. These external factors that distract us from eating purposefully include visual and auditory input that contribute to overload and short- circuit our perceptions of fullness.

Visual distractions can include a swirl of activity surrounding you in a crowded restaurant, or constantly passing multiple food items back and forth at a large table. Auditory distractions might include loud music in the background, or loud conversation from multiple people cross-talking. It is easy in these situations to lose track of how much food you are ingesting because you aren't visually keeping track of how much food goes on your plate or disappears from your plate. Consuming "food" at sports events or viewing such activity on television is the ultimate deception leading to extra food intake.

In a systematic review of 24 studies investigating the impact that distraction has on food intake, *The American Journal of Clinical Nutrition* observed how the consensus of the findings showed that a mindfulness approach of focused attention is important to lessen the impact of distractions. (See more about mindfulness techniques in the upcoming page.) Failing to be an attentive eater not only impacts consumption in the present, it affects later memories of consumption during subsequent meals, resulting in even more eating.

Robinson E. Et al. "Eating attentively: a systematic review and meta-analysis of the effect of food intake memory and awareness on eating." Am J Clin Nutr. 2013 April.

One consumption monitoring and mindfulness-based cue you might use in distracted eating situations involves 'crunching' and bite counting. Hearing yourself take bites and chewing seems to assist in controlling the amount of food you consume, according to research out of Brigham Young University in Utah. One study involved 71 test subjects who wore headphones as they ate pretzels out of bowls. Researchers fed loud white noise into half of the headphones, while the other half of participants heard the same white noise at a much softer level. Those given the loud noise consumed 45% more pretzels than the group who could hear themselves chewing the pretzels.

From these results the science team deduced that if you can hear yourself chewing, your attention will be more focused and you can more closely control how much you eat. Add to this monitoring cue a practice of counting how many bites you give each mouthful of food, and you will be engaged in a mindfulness practice with potential to manage your dietary habits via reduced consumption.

Elder RS. "The crunch effect: Food sound salience as a consumption monitoring cue." Food Quality & Preference. 2016 July.

Eat Too Fast, Gain More Weight

Eating too quickly can lead to eating more food and absorbing more calories than you intended to! The reason is that it takes about 20 minutes for the appetite center in the brain to receive the satiety signal that you've had enough and you no longer feel hungry. A fast eater overeats before the signal is sent, resulting in over-consumption.

Donald Altman, a psychotherapist, nationally-known mindful eating coach, and author of such books as Art of the Inner Meal, prepared this short quiz for us to give you to assess whether you need to slow down your eating.

Answer "yes" or "no" to the following questions:

1) Do you often feel "stuffed" after eating?

2) Do you normally eat your meals in less time than 20 minutes?

3) Do you watch TV while you eat dinner more often than not?

4) Does anyone ever comment that you inhale your food?

5) Do you feel after eating that you didn't really taste your food?

6) When eating with others, are you usually the first to finish eating?

If you answered "yes" to at least three or more of these, then you could benefit from slowing down your eating… and thereby eating less.

Time Your Food Intake for Weight Loss

If your goal is weight loss or maintenance in the long term, as it should be, the timing of when you eat can sometimes be almost as important as what you eat, according to scientific data.

To test the effect of timing on weight, a team of physiologists recruited 420 people who were overweight or obese and sorted them into two groups based on whether they were early eaters or late eaters. For 20 weeks, the participants had their vital signs and lifestyle habits monitored and evaluated.

Late eaters were defined as being more evening activity persons who had less desire for breakfasts or who skipped breakfast more frequently than early eaters. The timing of the main daily meal was also later in the day for those classified as late eaters.

It was clear at study's end that the late eaters were the biggest weight gainers compared to the earlier eaters. This finding prompted the science team to urge people seeking weight loss to pay closer attention to the timing of when they eat.

Why this weight difference between early and late eaters occurs seems to revolve around two factors: circadian rhythms and the nature of most nighttime activities.

In the case of circadian rhythms, these are mental and physical body changes over a 24-hour period influenced by the brain's master biological clock, which in turn is influenced by exposure to light. Dim light and flickering light from television, computer, and cell phone screens tend to alter this rhythm. Research has shown that these rhythms result in humans burning many more calories at 8 in the morning than at 8 in the evening. In fact, there seems to be an active circadian clock connected to food intake in different organs - the stomach, intestines, pancreas and liver.

Late eaters engage in watching television or computer screens more than early eaters. As a result, they are more prone to mindless eating, especially high-fat and sugary foods, which raises their calorie consumption counts. **Front-loading calories earlier in the day gives the body a greater chance of burning them off during the course of daily activities, whereas absorbing those calories later at night, before sleeping, means a slower metabolism gives the body more time to store calories as fat.**

More recent research has affirmed and expanded upon these findings. A 2022 study review out of Australia did an in-depth look at research findings on how humans metabolize calories during 24-hour periods, underscoring that night eating increases your risk of weight gain over time; two more reasons for weight gain, besides metabolism efficiency changes are "dysregulation of appetite hormone and gut microbiota by mistimed meals."

If you're a 'late night person' out of habit or inclination, and long-term weight loss is your goal, it may be time to read more books and watch less television and online computer content, and to post signs making the pantry and refrigerator off-limits past a certain hour of the evening. This is one of those little steps which can make a difference in calorie consumption---and your weight maintenance - over time.

Garaulet M. Et al. "Timing of food intake predicts weight loss effectiveness." Int J Obes. 2013 April.
"Davis R. Et al. "The Impact of Meal Timing on Risk of Weight Gain and Development of Obesity: a Review of the Current Evidence and Opportunities for Dietary Intervention." Curr Diab Rep. 2022 April.

Turn Down Your Stress Eating Dial

Scientific evidence indicates that chronic stress releases the hormone cortisol which signals your body to store more fat. The more stress you endure, the more fat your body will accumulate in response.

Not only that, but stress-releasing cortisol also stimulates cravings for consuming sugar or carbohydrates, which becomes another direct route to fat storage. As you can imagine, whatever you can do to relieve chronic stress in your life will help you with weight maintenance while achieving your weight reduction goals.

To calm your cortisol (stress) switch, adopting a mindfulness meditation practice would be quite helpful. In addition to that, any one of these three herbs might prove effective in stress relief: Rhodiola, Lemon balm, or Ashwagandha.

Rhodiola is a form of ginseng that has long been used in traditional ancient medical practices for stress relief.

Lemon balm, a mint, when dried and taken as a supplement, has a calming effect on the mind and body.

Ashwagandha is an herb used for thousands of years in the Ayurvedic medicine tradition of India as a calming agent. In a study involving 64 persons with chronic stress, this herb was given over a 60-day period (300 mg a day using a full-spectrum extract), and researchers concluded: "Ashwagandha root extract exhibited a significant reduction in scores on all stress-assessment scales and the serum cortisol levels were substantially reduced."

Kidd T. Et al. "The relationship between cortisol responses to laboratory stress and cortisol profiles in daily life." Biol Psych. 2014 February.
Chandrasekhar K. Et al. "A prospective, randomized double-blind, placebo-controlled study of safety and efficacy of high-concentration full-spectrum extract of ashwagandha root in reducing stress and anxiety in adults." Ind J Psych Med. 2012 July.

Transform 'Emotional Eating' into 'Intuitive Eating'

At the HeartMath Institute, a science research organization in California, scientists developed what they call 'The emWave Program for Stopping Emotional Eating,' designed to connect the core value of your heart to bring your emotions into balance and bring about habit changes that stop stress eating.

This program includes a series of easy exercises along with a CD and an emWave (stress reliever) device that aligns heart coherence to reduce stress hormones and food cravings. The underlying idea is that 'heart power' is different from willpower (exercising willpower can be stressful, whereas heart power balances hormones.)

In a series of steps, users learn to identify stress triggers and stress feelings, build internal coherence, reduce drama and connect to heart intelligence, and make a transition from emotional eating to intuitive eating. Some of the exercises involve focused attention breathing, a 'freeze frame' technique to take the drama out of reactions to situations, and an intuitive eating exercise to develop a sensitivity in the body to choose foods that are more nourishing to the body.

All of these are designed to help facilitate a sharpened ability to self-manage emotions to shut down cravings, food temptations, and emotional eating. For more information, go to our website, www.selfhealingdiet.com

Thirteen Fat Fighting Foods & Nutrients

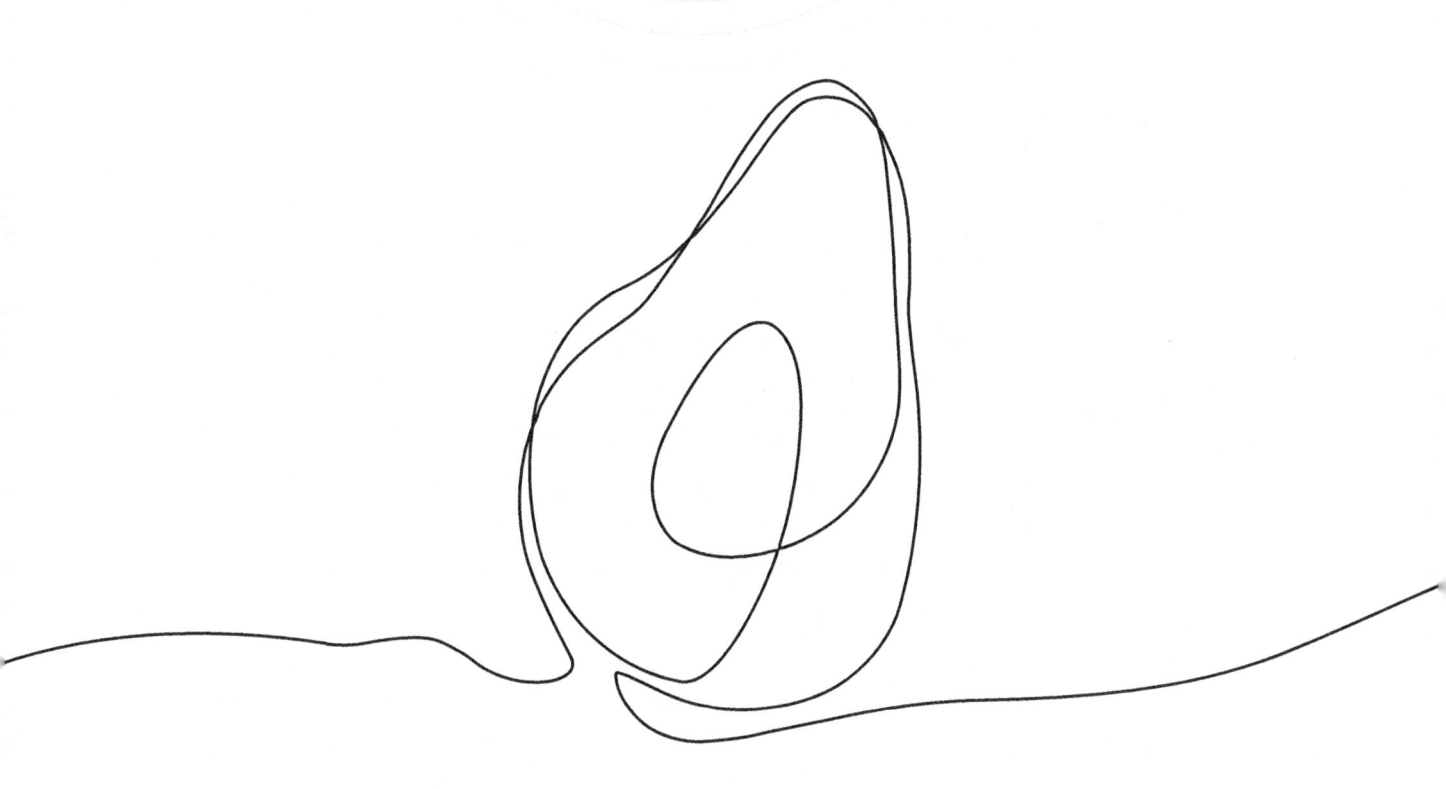

Sea Algae

Ocean plant life provides us with multiple unique nutrients to prevent or treat health conditions, including the discovery of a natural, non-drug treatment for being overweight and obese.

Some marine green algae species contain a chemical nutrient called siphonaxanthin, which assists the plant in absorbing green and blue light underwater, a function important to plant growth. This chemical was studied in 2014, and it was found to be a "novel functional compound."

A Japanese study using lab animals discovered that this chemical nutrient *could stop fat accumulation, and even more remarkably, it can alter the expression of genes that trigger the formation of fat cells.*

After six weeks, lab animals fed a 1.3 mg dose of siphonaxanthin each day experienced a white fat tissue reduction of 28%, along with a reduction of up to 95% in the activity of genes responsible for fat cell formation. This is good news for humans struggling with weight management. The benefits from consuming blue-green algae supplements, as well as other marine plants documented to contain this substance, make it an important addition to any long-term weight management plan.

Asian Ginseng

Known by numerous names - Panax ginseng, Korean ginseng, Chinese ginseng---this perennial plant from the mountains of eastern Asia is best known simply as Asian Ginseng, to differentiate it from American ginseng or Siberian ginseng. It's been a staple of Asian medicine traditions for thousands of years as a treatment for fatigue, depression, and a range of other symptoms, including obesity.

Some evidence has emerged from animal studies showing that eating ginseng can indeed therapeutically help fight obesity. In a study from 2017, published in the science journal, *Obesity*, green leaf and root extracts of Korean ginseng were administered to obese lab animals. Within weeks, the researchers could report that the ginseng "significantly decreased body weight and abdominal adipose tissue mass."

A year later, a second study of Korean ginseng appeared using lab animals who had been fed a high-fat diet until they were obese. They were then given eight weeks of supplementation with the ginseng, after which their body weights were assessed. There was clear evidence of decreased body weight, leading the science team to conclude: "ginseng may be able to prevent obesity."

Li ZS. Et al. "The green algal carotenoid siphonaxanthin inhibits adipogenesis in 3T3-L1 preadipocytes and the accumulation of lipids in white adipose tissue of KK-Ay mice." Journal of Nutrition. 2015 March.
Sugawara T. Et al. "Siphonaxanthin, a green algal carotenoid, as a novel functional compound." Marine Drugs. 2014 June.
Lee SG. Et al. "Panax ginseng Leaf Extracts Exert Anti-Obesity Effects in High-Fat Diet-Induced Obese Rats." Nutrients. 2017 September.

Ginger

As one of our most widely consumed spices, ginger has been around and used for enough centuries to have developed a reputation as a medicinal plant, particularly as an anti-inflammatory and digestive remedy. More recently, it has been studied for its ability to treat obesity and metabolic disorders.

A 2019 study, for example, examined its effects on lab animals after being fed a high-fat diet. After 16 weeks of ginger supplementation of 500 mg a day, those animals given this treatment decreased body weight and fat accumulation, compared to a control group fed the high-fat diet without ginger. The scientists doing the study concluded ginger altered the body's energy metabolism and induced the browning of white adipose fat, thus earning a reputation as "an edible plant that plays a role in the therapeutic treatment of obesity."

An earlier study in 2012, out of Columbia University, assessed the effects of ginger consumption on a group of overweight men, whose average age was 39 years. They were given two grams of ginger powder, dissolved in a hot water beverage, along with a breakfast meal each day. Every hour, feelings of satiety in the participants was assessed and blood samples were taken. Ginger reduced feelings of hunger, created a sense of fullness, and reduced later food intake. This finding led the science team to conclude the daily use of ginger as a supplement or food additive could be a useful tool in weight management.

Chia Seeds

Known to be filled with vitamins, minerals, fiber and antioxidants, chia seeds have the capacity, once digested, to prevent the absorption of some calories and foods, making it a useful and natural weight gain preventive as an addition to salads and most any meal.

Because chia seeds—thanks to the high levels of fiber--- absorb a dozen times their weight in water, consuming them also enhances feelings of fullness to help prevent overeating and food cravings. Their high levels of Omega-3 fatty acids assist in keeping blood sugar stabilized.

Studies done with athletes discovered that eating the seeds enhanced sports performance in endurance events, apparently due to the Omega-3 concentrations decreasing the dietary intake of sugars while increasing nutrient absorption for use as energy fuel. In simple terms, chia seed consumption slows down the human body's conversion and release of carbohydrates into the bloodstream.

Shin SS. Yoon M. "Korean red ginseng (Panax ginseng) inhibits obesity and improves lipid metabolism in high fat diet-fed castrated mice." J Ethnopharmacol. 2018 January. Wang J. Et al. "Ginger prevents obesity through regulation of energy metabolism and activation of browning in high-fat diet-induced obese mice." J Nutr Biochem. 2019 August. Mansour MS. Et al. "Ginger consumption enhances the thermic effect of food and promotes feelings of satiety without affecting metabolic and hormonal parameters in overweight men: a pilot study." Metabolism. 2012 October.

Avocado

Nutrient-dense avocados are a natural source of the 'good' fats needed for optimal health, including reaching your weight management goals. To illustrate their benefits, a study done at Loma Linda University found that test subjects who had a half of a fresh avocado with lunch each day reduced their later hunger by 40%, and this increased satiety helped reduce food consumption later in the day, thus reducing weight gain.

Apples/Pears

By eating three apples a day, or alternatively, three pears a day, a group of study volunteers were able to lose nearly three pounds more than a control group over 12 weeks. These findings resulted in a conclusion, published in the science journal, *Nutrition,* that apple or pear intake contributes to weight loss.

Shitake Mushrooms

Shiitake mushroom consumption provides numerous health benefits, given their anti- carcinogenic and immunity-stimulating effects on the human body. Because nutrients in these mushrooms are helpful in metabolizing fats, their use also becomes beneficial to contributing to reductions in body weight, according to a 2009 study by nutritional scientists.

Illian TG. Et al. "Omega 3 Chia seed loading as a means of carbohydrate loading." J Strength Cond Res. 2011 January.
Wien M. Et al. "A randomized 3x3 crossover study to evaluate the effect of Hass avocado intake on post-ingestive satiety, glucose and insulin levels, and subsequent energy intake in overweight adults. Nutr J. 2013 November.
De Oliveira M. Et al. "Weight loss associated with a daily intake of three apples or three pears among overweight women." Nutrition. 2003 March.
Rop O. Et al. "Beta-glucans in higher fungi and their health benefits." Nutr Rev. 2009 November.

Green Tea

Phytochemical combinations found in green tea have been the subject of numerous investigations into possible health benefits, one such area of inquiry being weight reduction and maintenance. In a 12-week clinical trial, using 240 volunteers, the science journal Obesity described how those who consumed the largest amounts of green tea had the greatest reductions in body fat, with an added benefit being lower blood pressure and LDL cholesterol. As a result, researchers recommended integrating green tea into diets as protection against obesity.

It's also beneficial to link your green tea consumption with exercise, drinking it before and after. In a 2019 study, published in the *British Journal of Clinical Pharmacology,* 30 overweight women were divided into three experimental groups: one combined endurance training with taking a placebo (sugar pill); the second did endurance training with taking 500 ml a day of green tea extract; while the third was a control group. The eight weeks of exercise consisted of three sessions per week of aerobics, fast walking, or jogging. At study's end, the green tea and exercise group had significantly reduced their body mass index and other fat measures compared to the other two groups.

Grapefruit

Numerous studies proved that grapefruit, if consumed as part of a regular dietary regimen, provides protection against obesity. A 2010 study, for example, identified nootkatone, a key nutrient in grapefruit, as a stimulator of enhanced energy metabolism to both improve physical performance and prevent weight gain. Another study, published in the *Journal of Medicinal Food,* examined the effects of grapefruit consumption in people with metabolic syndrome, that cluster of conditions including high blood pressure, high blood sugar, abnormal cholesterol, and excess body fat. All of these conditions improved in the patients who incorporated grapefruit into their weight reduction diet.

Nagao T. Et al. "A Green Tea Extract High in Catechins Reduces Body Fat and Cardiovascular Risk in Humans." Obesity. 2007 June.
Bagheri R. Et al. "Does Green Tea Extract Enhance the Anti-Inflammatory Effects of Exercise on Fat Loss?" Br J Clin Pharmacol. 2019 November.
Murase T. Et al. "Nootkatone, a characteristic of grapefruit, stimulates energy metabolism and prevent diet-induced obesity by activating AMPK." Am J Physiol Endocrinol Metab. 2010 August. Also, Fujioka K. Et al. "The effects of grapefruit on weight and insulin resistance: relationship to the metabolic syndrome." J Med Food. 2006.

Ashitaba

What is Ashitaba? You might ask. It's a species of perennial flowering plant, in the carrot family, which is native to Japan (botanists call it Angelica keiskei.) This phytochemical-rich herb has long been touted in Japanese culture as a health rejuvenator, a claim that scientists continue investigating.

In a 2019 study, a science team examined the health benefits of Ashitaba juice during a 10-week high-fat diet feeding program using lab animals. The results showed that supplementation with the juice prevented weight gain and lowered fat accumulation in the test animals, apparently because of how the phytochemical combination in the plant changed metabolic gene expression and gut microbiota.

Water & Lemons

A body of scientific evidence has emerged demonstrating that not only does increasing your water consumption help to flush toxins out of the body, but it also helps you to eat less, enhancing satiety before meals, as an effective weight loss and weight maintenance strategy. The key is to consume about 16 ounces of room-temperature water about 30 minutes before every meal, but don't drink it just before a meal or during a meal because that could interfere with digestion.

The American Journal of Clinical Nutrition published, in 2013, a systematic review of 13 studies examining the effects of drinking water as a dietary means for weight loss and obesity prevention. The overall evidence showed that increased water consumption reduced body weight after 3 to 12 months compared to no such increase in the 'control' study groups. "Studies of individuals dieting for weight loss or maintenance suggest a weight-reducing effect of increased water consumption," concluded the scientists involved in this study review.

Nutritionists at Virginia Tech University recruited 40 persons, average age of 63 years, and divided them into two groups: one group engaged in daily self-monitoring of body weight, step count, and fruit and vegetable intake; and a second group that did all of that monitoring along with consuming 16 ounces of water before each main meal and to record their water intake. The study lasted for 12 months. At its conclusion, the researchers found the addition of water consumption and water use monitoring had produced more weight loss in that study group, prompting the observation that drinking water before each meal provides effective weight-loss maintenance if used as a practice over long periods of time.

Zhang C. Et al. "Daily Supplementation with Fresh Angelica keiskei Juice Alleviates High-Fat Diet-Induced Obesity in Mice by Modulating Gut Microbiota Composition." Mol Nutr Food Res. 2019 June.
Muckelbauer R. Et al. "Association between water consumption and body weight outcomes: a systematic review." Am J Clin Nutr. 2013 August.

Another benefit of water consumption before meals was uncovered by scientists in Germany, who observed the dietary habits of 1,987 schoolchildren. Those children who consumed sugar-containing beverages (soft drinks and juices) increased their body mass index over the course of a school year, whereas the children who increased their water consumption did not. This replacement of sugary beverages with pure water consumption helped to prevent obesity.

To increase the fat burn and fat prevention powers of water, add lemon! The negative charge and polyphenols of lemon makes water electrically active, which helps with body detoxification, preventing overeating, aiding with metabolism and digestion, and assisting with keeping the excess weight off. (You might also consider adding ginger to your water since it helps to control appetite.)

As an illustration of the powers of lemon water, Japanese scientists divided lab animals into three groups: one fed a low-fat diet, a second fed a high-fat diet, and the third fed a high-fat diet supplemented with lemon polyphenols extracted from lemon peel. The experiment lasted 12 weeks. At the end, the third group consuming the lemon was found to have its body weight gain and fat accumulations "significantly suppressed," the science team reported, showing the potential of lemon to aid in weight loss.

A Korean research study placed 84 premenopausal women into three groups: a control group without diet restriction, a group fed a 'placebo' diet, and a lemon juice detox diet group. After 11 days of evaluation and measurements of each group's body weight, body mass index, percentage of body fat, and waist-hip ratio, positive changes were seen in all those measurements for the lemon detox group participants, leading the scientists to conclude that a lemon juice detox reduces body fat and would be helpful in any weight loss program.

Akers JD. Et al. "Daily self-monitoring of body weight, step count, fruit/vegetable intake, and water consumption: a feasible and effective long-term weight loss maintenance approach." J Acad Nutr Diet. 2012 May.
Muckelbauer R. Et al. "Changes in water and sugar-containing beverage consumption and body weight outcomes in children." Br J Nutr. 2016 June.
Fukuchi Y. Et al. "Lemon Polyphenols Suppress Diet-induced Obesity by Up-Regulation of mRNA Levels of the Enzymes Involved in B-Oxidation in Mouse White Adipose Tissue." J Clin Bioc Nutr. 2008.
Kim MJ. Et al. "Lemon detox diet reduced body fat, insulin resistance, and serum hs-CRP level without hematological changes in overweight Korean women." Nutrition Research. 2015 May.

Plant-Based Supplements Melt Abdominal Fat

Abdominal fat, otherwise known as visceral obesity, is a 'dysfunctional subcutaneous adipose tissue expansion' that we often characterize in common conversation as 'beer belly' or 'Buddha belly' or just 'a big gut.' More than any other fat region of the body, this one area is most responsible for hypertriglyceridemia, the release of proinflammatory cytokines, liver insulin resistance and inflammation, presence of LDL particles and reduced HDL cholesterol levels. These are all factors contributing to the serious health condition called metabolic syndrome.

One important contributing factor to the accumulation of abdominal fat seems to be diminishing AMPK, an enzyme that serves as an energy sensor in body cells. AMPK activity diminishes with age, resulting in weight gain, particularly around the midsection, so scientists have experimented with ways to boost AMPK production.

A medicinal herb extract from traditional Chinese medicine, Actiponin, has been found to activate AMPK and help slow or even shut down fat production, as well as accelerate the body's burning of fat. Using 80 overweight test subjects, Korean scientists divided them randomly into an Actiponin intervention group (receiving 450 mg a day), and a placebo control group receiving a sugar pill. During the 12-week clinical trial, the test subjects were constantly monitored.

At study's end, "total abdominal fat area, body weight, body fat mass, percent body fat, and BMI (body mass index) were significantly decreased in the Actiponin group compared to the placebo group," concluded the science team, writing in the science journal, Obesity. No adverse side effects emerged from the Actiponin supplementation.

Tchernof A. Despres JP. "Pathophysiology of human visceral obesity: an update." Physiol Rev. 2013 January.

Abdominal fat was reduced by 11% over the 12-week study period in the test subjects receiving the extract, while their total fat area was reduced by 6.3%, compared to the placebo group. These are important results supporting Actiponin's weight reduction and safety potential.

A second extract discovered to activate AMPK production is hesperidin, a citrus flavonoid. In a clinical study done at the University of Rome, Italy, Department of Internal Medicine, volunteers with metabolic syndrome were given 500 mg once a day for three weeks. Their metabolic symptoms and levels of inflammation were monitored and measured. When the study ended, it was clear that hesperidin supplementation reduced inflammation and improved vascular function in ways that contributed to abdominal fat reduction. The results were considered comparable to effects from metformin, a prescription drug given to activate AMPK and regulate fat storage. Unlike metformin, which induces side effects in some people, hesperidin appears safe and easily tolerated.

Here at Hippocrates Wellness, we have developed our own proprietary blend and created *Melt Away Weight Loss,* **an enzyme complex that offers a safe and proven way to help the body eliminate unwanted fats.** The enzymes, lipase and amylase, assist the digestive and eliminative systems in their quest to rid the body of excess lipids. This formulation contains powerful herbs which work in the human body by helping regulate the metabolism of glucose, fat cells, and muscle cells. These herbs help reduce glucose absorption in the gastrointestinal tract and increase combustion in fat cells and glycogen synthesis in the muscle cells. They also decrease circulating glucose and reduce fat accumulation, resulting in a favorable metabolic environment for correcting and supporting Type 2 Diabetic conditions. Other benefits include decreased appetite, hunger and cravings, and increased fat burning, fat loss and insulin sensitivity.

Park SH. Et al. "Antiobesity effect of Gynostemma pentaphyllum extract (actiponin): a randomized, double-blind, placebo-controlled trial." Obesity. 2014 January.
Rizza S. Et al. "Citrus polyphenol hesperidin stimulates production of nitric oxide in endothelial cells while improving endothelial function and reducing inflammatory markers in patients with metabolic syndrome." J Clin Endocrinol Metab. 2011 May.

End Cravings Using Spinach, Peppers & Cinnamon

Scientists aren't sure why, but the thylakoids (chlorophyll membranes) found abundantly in spinach affect areas of the human brain involved with receiving signals for food cravings. Once consumed, spinach disrupts these cravings signals enough to give many people relief from unhealthy food urges.

Swedish scientists at Lund University tested spinach consumption on a group of overweight women volunteers in 2015 and found the following: the thylakoids in spinach reduced hunger by 21%, increased feelings of fullness (satiety) by 14%, reduced cravings for snacks and sweets during the day by 36%, and reduced cravings for salty foods by 30% making spinach consumption a highly effective deterrent to overeating and weight gain.

A second study from the same team of researchers recruited 20 overweight women and gave them breakfast meals with or without the spinach thylakoids and took blood samples from each woman over a four-hour period afterward. Those women who ate the spinach were able to suppress food cravings for more than three hours after ingesting it, showing the power of spinach to repress cravings.

Capsaicin, taken from **red peppers**, and also EGCG (epigallocatechin-3-gallate) found in **green tea**, have been documented to have effects on restraining appetite and controlling food cravings.

At Maastricht University, in Holland, scientists recruited 27 average-weight men and women to test combinations of capsaicin capsules, sweet pepper capsules (CH-19 sweet pepper from Thailand), and a green tea drink on appetite, satiety, and cravings. These ingredients in various combinations were consumed with meals.

Stenblom EL. Et al. "Consumption of thylakoid-rich spinach extract reduces hunger, increases satiety and reduces cravings for palatable food in overweight women." Appetite. 2015 August.
Stenblom EL. Et al. "Supplementation by thylakoids to a high carbohydrate meal decreases feelings of hunger, elevates CCK levels and prevents postprandial hypoglycaemia in overweight women." Appetite. 2013 September.

Over ten days the volunteers had their appetite, body weight, energy intake and heart rate measured. Of the various combinations tested, capsaicin capsules consumed with green tea significantly reduced the desire to eat fatty and salty foods.

To do this on your own, you might drink a glass of green tea and take two 250-milligram capsules of capsaicin before you start your day.

A synergism of bioactive ingredients is the active principle here, since these ingredients interact within the body to reduce energy intake needs, thus making you feel fuller and reducing your appetite.

For thousands of years, **cinnamon,** from the bark of a small evergreen tree, has been touted as having medicinal properties. More recently, science teams have demonstrated how the ingestion of cinnamon controls blood glucose levels, preventing insulin from spiking after eating a meal. This normalizes blood sugar, making a person less likely to crave sugar.

Ball State University scientists in Indiana, worked with 30 volunteers, between 18 and 30 years of age, including both normal-weight and obese adults. After eating six grams of ground cinnamon with a cereal in the morning, they had their blood glucose levels measured periodically over two hours. The cinnamon was effective, with both obese and normal-weight persons, in keeping their blood glucose levels in check.

A second study done by nutritional scientists using 22 male and female volunteers combined ground cinnamon, ginger, and green tea to test blood glucose levels. This combination had synergistic effects, normalizing blood sugar levels much more potently than any herb could do by itself.

Cinnamon contains the chemicals cinnamaldehyde, cinnamyl acetate, and cinnamyl alcohol, which together act to neutralize spikes in blood sugar levels after the ingestion of food. You might try using it before meals or shopping to reduce the temptation to buy or eat sugary foods.

Reinbach HC. Et al. "Effects of capsaicin, green tea and CH-19 sweet pepper on appetite and energy intake in humans in negative and positive energy balance." Clinical Nutrition. 2009 June. Also, Westerterp-Plantenga M. Et al. "Metabolic effects of spices, teas, and caffeine." Physiology & Behavior. 2006 August.
Azzeh FS."Synergistic effect of green tea, cinnamon and ginger combination on enhancing postprandial blood glucose." Also, Pakistan Journal of Biological Science. 2013 January. Also, Magistrelli A. Chezem JC."Effect of ground cinnamon on postprandial blood glucose concentration in normal-weight and obese adults." Journal of the Academy of Nutrition Diet. 2012 November.

Action Tip: Put Your Focus on Food Quality

One technique for healthful eating, focusing your priorities on food quality rather than food quantity, involves devoting five minutes a day to a short reflection on a small food item. This can be done before a meal as a weight-watching exercise.

Known as The Raisin Meditation, it was developed by mindfulness expert Jon Kabat Zinn, a professor of Medicine at the University of Massachusetts Medical School. He used a raisin, but for our purposes, you can use a walnut or a chia seed.

1. Hold. Take the small food item and hold it between your thumb and finger.

2. See. Gaze at the food item with your full attention. Pretend that you have never really examined this item in detail before. Explore every part of it and admire its unique features.

3. Touch. Turn the item between your fingers. Do this with your eyes closed to enhance the feeling of touch.

4. Smell. Hold the item close to your nose and inhale the aroma. Whatever the smell, notice what sensations this triggers in your mouth or in your stomach.

5. Closer. Bring the food item close to your lips. Do this slowly. Then gently place the item in your mouth. Don't chew. Just focus on the sensation of it in your mouth or on your tongue.

6. Taste. Slowly with awareness, take a couple of gentle bites into the food item. Don't swallow yet. Just savor it in your mouth and pay attention to the consistency of it.

7. Swallow. When you are ready to swallow it, do so slowly and deliberately. Feel it descend inside you.

8. Feeling. Notice the sensations that emerge for you as the food item moves down into your stomach. What is the aftertaste in your mouth? Imagine yourself becoming satiated at the completion of this exercise.

Action Tip: Mindful Eating for Weight Control

Psychotherapist Donald Altman offers some easy meal-time ideas to slow down and eat moderately by getting in touch with your hunger signals.

1) Play some calming and soothing music that lasts from 20 or 25 minutes. Pace the eating to the music and end your meal when the music ends.

2) Pay attention to how many times you chew your food. Try to chew each bite for as many as 10 times. As you do this, pay attention to the taste and texture of the food as it changes from solid to liquid in your mouth.

3) Get in the habit of leaving some food on your plate (eating them as leftovers later). By giving yourself permission to leave some food, you can break old habits of needing to "clean your plate" and eat more than you need.

Action Tip: Turn Meal Choices into a Health Ritual

When we ritualize our mealtimes, paying awareness and giving appreciation to all aspects of the meal preparation and consumption process, we give free attention to everything that is important about our food habits, other than just eating large quantities of it as fast as possible. Taking a series of mindful steps helps us to eat smarter so we weigh less.

Here are the steps:

1. **Ask yourself,** am I eating because I am hungry, or am I simply being impulsive.

2. **Ask yourself,** is the food I have chosen truly healthy and nutritious for me. If you have doubts, choose something else.

3. **Make certain** you are focused on the food prepared for the meal before you, rather than be distracted by television, cell phones, and the like. Turn them off!

4. **Give yourself** a few minutes to reflect on the origin of the food you are about to consume. Where does it come from? Visualize how it was grown and how it was transported to your table. Express silent or verbal gratitude for all of these steps in the meal process.

5. **Next,** feel your appreciation for whoever prepared the meal. Give thanks for the role they are playing in giving you and others sustenance.

6. **While eating,** do so slowly and mindfully. Take your time to chew each bite thoroughly. Do not swallow your food whole.

7. **Visualize** yourself absorbing this food and transforming it into the energy you need to live your daily life and remain healthy.

8. **Visualize** yourself at the weight you desire to be…with a wide smile on your face.

Body Tune-Ups for Weight Health

Super Immunity for Weight Control

Your immune system plays more of a role in your body's weight management than you may suspect. It generally works like this: Your diet and your mind, with its beliefs and attitudes, and emotions, influences the functioning of your immune system, that defense network designed to heal your body. Part of that healing process involves keeping your body at its optimal weight.

In case you only have a vague idea of what your immune system involves, here are some of the important elements in this vast network of cells, organs, and tissues. There are groups of cells (T cells, B cells, and NK cells) produced in bone marrow which then circulate through the bloodstream to fight off pathogen invaders; and then there is the lymphatic system with the lymph nodes, and the spleen, the tonsils, the appendix, and the microbiome living in the intestines. Though we are all born with some level of immunity, it's with aging and experience that the immune system adapts to exposure to pathogens and diseases and develops a memory for how to fight off threats.

An unhealthy diet deficient in certain nutrients directly affects the strength of your immune system, as do negative thoughts, beliefs, and emotions. In the case of diet, if you fail to consume enough non-meat foods, you don't absorb a sufficient range of nutrients to keep your immune system functioning at high capacity. These vital nutrients include vitamin C, vitamin D., zinc, selenium, iron, and proteins (all of which can be derived from plant sources). What further depresses your immune system, inviting the development of disease, is excess weight and obesity, which triggers

"How the immune system works." MedicalNewsToday. www.medicalnewstoday.com/articles/320101

inflammatory responses in the body that cause the immune system to go into overdrive and get worn out over time.

One obvious example of the mind having an effect on the immune system (in this case, a negative effect) is something most of us have experienced - chronic stress. When you worry constantly, when you are under unrelenting pressure from the challenges of work and life, you release the hormones cortisol and adrenaline into your bloodstream, which suppress your immune responses. For many people, with chronic worry comes chronic overeating and overconsumption of alcohol, making matters even worse for your body weight and your immune system efficiency.

By some medical authority estimates, fully half of all deaths in the world today are attributable to inflammation-related diseases that immune systems are too depleted to adequately heal. These diseases include diabetes, heart disease, stroke, cancer, and metabolic disorders triggered by excess weight. This stark reality provides us with a clarion call for taking firmer control of our health choices as sovereign individuals.

To develop Super Immunity naturally, to rejuvenate and protect both your body and mind, you need to make science-backed decisions that empower yourself, without a reliance on quick-fix diets and pharmaceutical drugs. "There are now several lines of research," observed an article on immunity in *Scientific American*, "suggesting that our mental perception of the world constantly informs and guides our immune system in a way that makes us better able to respond to future threats."

One of those lines of scientific research revolves around the use of mind power for healing, triggered by placebos. Another body of research focuses on mind power for supporting the immune system, using mindfulness meditation. Because placebos use inert substances like water masquerading as drugs, many scientists and physicians call placebos fake treatments, but they really aren't fake if they are effective at triggering healing. Dr. Joseph Dispenza devoted an entire book, *You Are the Placebo: Making Your Mind Matter,* to documenting how it's possible to heal ourselves using our thoughts alone. If we believe a placebo is a self-healing effect and can help to heal us, even when we know it is only the power of suggestion at work, more often than not, the placebo will have a beneficial effect as a result of our beliefs and expectations. Placebos have been shown to positively influence physiological functions ranging from our immune system response to managing our hormone levels. Much more research needs to be done on the placebo. We believe it is possible that the placebo effect is itself self-healing.

"Nutrition and Immunity." Harvard T.H. Chan School of Public Health. www.hsph.harvard.edu/nutritionsource/nutrition-and-immunity/
"Chronic inflammation in the etiology of disease across the life span." Furman D. Et al. Nat Med. 2019 December.
"The Science of Healing Thoughts." Jo Marchant. Scientific American. January 19, 2016.

With mindfulness meditation, a large body of research over the past two decades demonstrates a positive link between this mind practice and strengthening the immune system, resulting in supporting a healthy weight. Scientists writing in the *Annals of the New York Academy of Sciences,* in 2016, reviewed the findings from 20 clinical studies investigating the effects of mindfulness meditation on the immune system. This review evaluated five biological outcomes as measured in the studies: **1)** *circulating and stimulated inflammatory proteins,* **2)** *cellular transcription factors and gene expression,* **3)** *immune cell count, 4) immune cell aging,* **5)** *antibody response. This study review discovered measurable positive effects from meditation showing up on all five outcomes tracking immune system dynamics.*

Still another study of meditation and immunity surfaced more recently, in 2022, from scientists in Spain and the U.S., who observed 28 participants in a month-long meditation retreat in California. Blood samples were taken from the participants on day two of the retreat and again three weeks later. These blood results measuring immune system parameters were then compared against a control group of people who didn't attend the retreat. What the scientists found was clear evidence that the meditators had boosted their immune system functions significantly, changing the expression of several genes involved with inflammation and positively influencing other inflammatory mechanisms.

These 'mind over body' study results should be taken to heart---and become a lifestyle practice - if you truly want to dedicate yourself to achieving and sustaining an optimal healthy weight using the self-healing diet.

"Mindfulness meditation and the immune system: a systematic review of randomized controlled trials." Black DS. Slavich GM. Ann NY Acad Sci. 2016 June. "Changes in the expression of inflammatory and epigenetic-modulatory genes after an intensive meditation retreat." Alvarez-Lopez MJ. Et al. Compr Psychoneuroendocrinol. 2022 June. Alvarez-Lopez MJ. Et al. Compr Psychoneuroendocrinol. 2022 June.

How Your Diet & Gut Microbes Interact

It's one of those proverbial vicious cycles. Having excess weight on your body contributes to low-grade chronic inflammation, and in turn, this chronic inflammation impairs your immune system and gut health, which results in a contribution to more rapid weight gain. It's a cycle that must be broken if long-term healthy weight maintenance is to be achieved.

Let's start with your immune system. Much of that protective system resides in the intestines, usually called the gut. The entire traditional Western diet has become a risk factor for developing chronic inflammation and with it, obesity. (Chronic inflammation is an over-response by the immune system to perceived threats.)

Deficiencies of zinc, selenium, iron, copper, and folic acid in your diet can compromise your immune system responses. Low levels of vitamins A, B6, C, D and E can also affect your overall immune system efficiency. A well-rounded plant-based diet provides all these nutrients for immunity, helping to protect you from bacterial, viral, and other types of infections. One of the most powerful immune boosters among food groups is garlic.

You've probably seen this phenomenon among your family and friends. After eating the same meals, consuming similar food portions, some people will gain more weight than others. Science research tells us it has to do with whose gut is more efficient at extracting calories from the foods. That efficiency at calorie extraction and conversion depends on the diversity of the microbes in our intestines and how much inflammation our immune system allows to affect this microbiome.

Childs CE Et al. "Diet and Immune Function." Nutrients. 2019 August.
"How Does Nutrition Affect the Immune System?" Theresa Houghton. T. Colin Campbell Center for Nutrition Studies. March 20, 2020.

Our gut microbes play a real but often unacknowledged role in weight gain. This connection first became apparent a few decades ago, in animals, when cows given antibiotics grew larger more quickly than animals not receiving antibiotics. Subsequent research determined that the antibiotics were exterminating some types of gut microbes that assist the livestock in food digestion by slowing down weight gain. A similar process occurs in humans. By decreasing the diversity of microbes in the human microbiome - a result of a nutrient-deficient diet, or by weakening the immune system, which is helping to control diversity in the gut microbiome - humans open the door to unwanted weight gain because they have reduced the numbers of beneficial gut bacteria which help to keep weight in check. This microbe deficiency underscores the growing popularity of probiotic supplements. It also explains why some physicians recommend that patients take probiotics after receiving prescriptions for antibiotics and some other types of drugs.

A more natural and efficient way to replenish your microbiome, maintain healthy colonies of bacteria, and assist your immune system function, and combat weight gain, is to regularly eat generous portions of probiotic foods such as fermented vegetables, sauerkraut, tempeh, kimchi, and miso. (To test the types of bacteria in your biome, so you will have a better idea of how to replenish the types you need and lack, go to our website, www.selfhealingdiet.com, where you will find at-home test kits.)

Also, as pointed out by the Harvard School of Public Health, "A high-fiber plant-rich diet with plenty of fruits, vegetables, whole grains, and legumes appears to support the growth and maintenance of beneficial microbes. Certain helpful microbes break down fibers into short-chain fatty acids, which have been shown to stimulate immune cell activity."

We now know, thanks to recent scientific findings, that the human microbial community within our intestines plays an important role in human health and by extension, in maintaining a healthy body weight. We also are learning that the human biome, as those gut microbes are called, has direct connections to the ancient microbes in soil and thus to the plant microbial and immune systems which provide the conduit between soil and we humans.

Three soil scientists at the University of Natural Resources and Life Sciences, in Austria, published a pioneering study in 2019, appearing in the science journal, *Microorganisms,* in which they noted how we should "consider the human intestinal microbiome as well as the soil/root microbiome as 'superorganisms' which, by close contact, replenish each other with inoculants, genes, and growth-sustaining molecules."

"The Fundamental Link Between Body Weight and the Immune System." James Hamblin. The Atlantic. August 2, 2019.
"Nutrition and Immunity." Harvard School of Public Health. www.hsph.harvard.edu/nutritionsource/nutrition-and-immunity/

> "From early childhood," their study paper continued, "we are in contact with soil; we taste it, we inhale it, and we drink water which has passed through soil. Moreover, we ingest plants grown on soils together with soil microbiota... As human activities are changing the distribution and abundance of soil microorganisms, e.g., by agricultural land use, the resultant changes in microbial ecosystems may not only affect biogeochemical cycles but also human health."

Aside from gastrointestinal diseases, research is finding a direct link between our gut health and the plants, their dependence on the soils, and the onset and acceleration of obesity and metabolic syndrome. As unhealthy foods diminish our intestinal microorganism diversity and numbers, our bad dietary choices break the links forged by evolution that bind our health to that of our soils and the plants dependent on those soils.

By acknowledging that our intestinal microbial population influences our health, and that this population is reliant on soil and plant microorganisms, we begin to see the bigger picture of linkages and interactions and we do so from a new perspective, taking into account the broader impacts of climate change in disrupting this balance shaped over eons of evolution in its natural wisdom.

Most people don't realize that plants possess complex immune systems that are "similar to the innate immune systems of humans," according to a study by plant biologists at Michigan State University. Plants have evolved surveillance and defensive systems to respond to their environment, particularly when that environment changes drastically due to drought or other environmental influences. As a result, noted the plant scientists, "epidemics in ecosystems are rare, and when they do occur, they are typically restricted to a specific geographical region, climate, or a combination of both." The wildcard factor, however, disrupting this balance, has been interference by humans that destroy wide swaths of ecosystems.

We believe that further scientific investigations of the relationship between the soil biome, the plant biome and the human biome will provide important information giving us another key to optimal

Blum WEH Et al. "Does Soil Contribute to the Human Gut Microbiome?" Microorganisms. 2019 September.

health. Compounds called humic/fulvic acids are derived from the decomposition of dead plant and animal matter and are essential to the health of the world's soils. Experiments with lab animals revealed that supplementation with humic/fulvic acids resulted in strong immune system stimulation.

Testing of a traditional medicine called Moomiaii, used for over 3,000 years in India and China, with its main constituents being humic/fulvic acids, found it a safe dietary supplement for treating diabetes and other diseases. Still another substance, Shilajit, found in the Himalayas and Hindukush mountain ranges, contains a mixture of humic/fulvic acids and has been used for thousands of years as a rejuvenator and antioxidant

Adding humic/fulvic back into the soil will be necessary as part of the long-term solutions to climate change.

Li P. Et al. "The Lifecycle of the Plant Immune System." CRC Crit Rev Plant Science. 2020.
"A toxicological evaluation of a fulvic and humic acids preparation." Murbach TS. Et al. Toxicol Rep. 2020 September 14. Also, "Effect of fulvic and humic acids on performance, immune response and thyroid function in rats." Vucskits AV. Et al. J Anim Physiol Anim Nutr. 2010 December. Also, "Health Beneficial Effects of Moomiaii in Traditional Medicine." Barouji SR. Et al. Galen Med J. 2020 August 27. Also, "Shilajit: a review." Agarwal SP. Et al. Phytother Res. 2007 May.

Don't Overlook the Importance of Phytochemicals

As part of their immune systems' defensive response to insects and bacterial and fungal pathogens, plants produce a wide range of phytochemicals, an estimated 8,000 different types. Many of these phytochemicals, in turn, confer significant antioxidant health benefits on humans when ingested, offering protection against certain cancers and cardiovascular disease, as well as retarding the free radical damage that leads to premature aging.

Having regular infusions of phytochemicals in your diet provides still another proven health benefit - they help you to lose weight or maintain a healthy weight. Dutch scientists, for example, found that women with the highest intake of several types of phytochemicals - flavonols/flavones and catechins - experienced "significantly lower increases in body weight" over a period of years compared to women who didn't embrace a plant-based diet.

Polyphenols play a big fat fighter role. In a meta-analysis (comparison of multiple science studies) released in 2023, results from 40 clinical trials were analyzed showing that dietary polyphenols (found in plant-based foods from nuts to onions) showed statistically significant reductions in body weight, body mass index and waist circumference in human test subjects. Further analysis found that these positive weight and body changes persisted beyond three months when dosages were kept in the range of 220 mg per day, indicating the long term potential for the prevention and management of obesity.

"The effectiveness of dietary polyphenols in obesity management: A systematic review and meta-analysis of human clinical trials." Zhang Y. Et al. Food Chemistry. 2023 March.

A natural flavonoid, Kaempferol, found in some fruits and vegetables such as broccoli, was affirmed in a study to regulate both energy metabolism and inflammation in the body in ways that help to fight weight gain and obesity. In this 2023 animal study, obese adult mice received kaempferol for 40 days and had their inflammation and energy balance monitored. At the end of treatment significant body weight loss was observed, along with reduced fasting blood glucose and insulin sensitivity, showing the potential that exists in humans for similar positive results from regular kaempferol consumption.

"Dietary flavonoid kaempferol reduces obesity-associated hypothalamic microglia activation and promotes body weight loss in mice with obesity." Romero-Juarez PA. Et al. Nutri Neuroscience. 2023 January.
Altemimi A. Et al. "Phytochemicals: Extraction, Isolation, and Identification of Bioactive Compounds from Plant Extracts." Plants. 2017 December.
Hughes LA. Et al. "Higher dietary flavones, flavonol, and catechin intakes are associated with less of an increase in BMI over time in women: a longitudinal analysis from the Netherlands Cohort Study." Am J Clin Nutrition. 2008.

Reverse Insulin Resistance

As you learned in Part One, insulin resistance contributes to weight gain.

If you are diagnosed with insulin resistance, Dr. Lara Briden suggests this strategy for insulin resistance reversal: build muscle with weight training, avoid all ultra-processed foods, consume sufficient quality protein, address any underlying gut problems (because gut inflammation worsens insulin resistance), get enough sleep, reduce stress, and eat the same time every day.

We can add to her prescription for insulin resistance reversal the following:

- Do regular immersion in saunas and hot tubs. Study evidence shows that using saunas and hot tubs for 30 minutes a day, six days a week, increases the circulation of free fatty acids, a process helpful to reducing insulin resistance, while triggering the body to break up fat deposits.

- Consume regular helpings of grapefruit. Numerous studies of grapefruit and weight loss turned up findings of positive impacts on insulin resistance and obesity from regular grapefruit consumption, owing to a grapefruit nutrient (nootkatone) which enhances the body's energy metabolism.

"The Most Common Cause of Weight Gain." Lara Briden. May 11, 2022. https://www.larabriden.com/the-most-common-cause-of-weight-gain/

McCarty MF. Et al. "Regular thermal therapy may promote insulin sensitivity while boosting expression of endothelial nitric oxide synthase—effects comparable to those of exercise training." Med Hypotheses. 2009 July.

Fujioka K. Et al. "The effects of grapefruit on weight and insulin resistance: relationship to the metabolic syndrome." J Med Food. 2006.

Post-Meal Strolls Control Blood Sugar

You must know by now that the more sedentary you are, especially from prolonged sitting in front of a television, a mobile device, or computer screen, the more likely you are to gain unwanted weight and simultaneously, raise your risk for type 2 diabetes and other negative health conditions. The scientific evidence - and just plain common sense - informs us that our total time spent every day being sedentary expands our waistline while shortening our life.

An often overlooked yet effective intervention shows up in the habits of people in Mediterranean countries who have traditionally adhered to the Mediterranean diet. After each meal, these people generally take short walks to meeting places and socialize with friends and neighbors. Now scientific studies have affirmed a critical factor in how and why this activity proves beneficial to health - post-meal strolls lower blood sugar.

Five scientists writing in the science journal, *Sports Medicine,* did an analysis contrasting the results from seven independent studies that examined the impacts on glucose (blood sugar) and insulin from sitting, standing and walking. Each of the seven studies had test participants either standing or walking for two to five minutes, every half-hour or so, during the course of their waking hours. The *Sports Medicine* findings, published in 2022, showed that "intermittent standing breaks throughout the day and after meals reduced glucose on average by 9.5% compared to prolonged sitting. However, intermittent light intensity walking produced a greater reduction of glucose by an average of 17% compared to prolonged sitting."

Just two minutes of walking right after eating had measurable beneficial effects on blood sugar levels. Walking helps to counteract the large spikes in blood sugar that most people experience after consuming food, which usually occurs within an hour to 90 minutes after finishing the meal. Because our muscles need glucose to function, body movements such as walking assist us in cleaning sugars from our bloodstream and that in turn, helps us to keep excess weight off.

The longer and more vigorously you walk after a meal, the greater you 'prime' your metabolism to burn excess calories, a process which exacts cumulative positive effects on both weight and overall health in the long-term.

Buffey AJ. Et al. "The Acute Effects of Interrupting Prolonged Sitting Time in Adults with Standing and Light-Intensity Walking on Biomarkers of Cardiometabolic Health in Adults: A Systematic Review and Meta-Analysis." Sports Medicine. 2022 February 11.

Put Your Hormones Back in Balance

Medical surveys show that obesity is more prevalent in women than in men, which is true both in the U.S. and globally. While the temptation might be to assume much of the reason for this disparity involves hormonal differences between the sexes, as you will see in this section, that is only partly true, since men face their own hormonal and weight gain challenges thanks to the impact aging has on testosterone.

What complicates the situation for women is their longer life expectancy. "Since women in developed countries live approximately one-third of their lives after menopause, and 68% of U.S. women in the 40 to 59-year age group are overweight or obese, understanding factors that influence body fat and its distribution in relation to the menopause transition is of critical importance," concluded a 2008 study, published in the *International Journal of Obesity*.

A primary reason for weight gain and obesity in women can be attributed to the wide fluctuations in their sex hormones, occurring during and after menopause, that are more severe than what most men encounter. Here is what the science journal, *Biomed Research International*, had to say in 2014, about the origins of obesity during menopause: "A growing body of evidence now demonstrates that estrogenic signaling can have an important role in obesity development in menopausal women. Menopausal women are three times more likely to develop obesity and metabolic syndrome abnormalities than premenopausal women. Furthermore, estrogen/progestin-based hormone replacement therapy in menopausal women has been shown to lower visceral adipose tissue."

Lovejoy JC Et al. "Increased visceral fat and decreased energy expenditure during the menopausal transition." Int J Obesity. 2008.
Lizcano F. Guzman G. "Estrogen Deficiency and the Origin of Obesity during Menopause." Biomed Res Int. 2014.

In an analysis of 107 clinical trials of hormone replacement therapy (HRT) in postmenopausal women, Stanford University School of Medicine scientists found that HRT reduced abdominal fat by an average of 6.8% in participants in studies that lasted at least eight weeks. Oral HRT agents were found to produce larger beneficial effects than HRT from transdermal agents.

Not only does a woman's estrogen and progesterone levels decline after menopause, but so does her androgen production. (Yes, like men, women have androgens, the most prominent being testosterone; they just exhibit them in much lower levels than men.) In a 16-week study involving 40 postmenopausal women, average age of 57 years, it was found that estrogen plus androgen replacement therapy increased lean body mass while decreasing fat mass more than estrogen therapy alone did. Body fat declined by an average of 7.4% among study participants over the four-month period, and "there were no noteworthy side effects," reported the researchers. Additionally, they pointed to other research findings that "androgen therapy in conjunction with diet and exercise demonstrated efficacy in reducing abdominal fat and weight in postmenopausal women with unexplained weight gain."

As further evidence of hormone replacement therapy impact, a group of 1,053 postmenopausal women, aged 50 to 80 years, were assessed over a 10-year period, with periodic measurements of their body fat, based on whether they were current users of menopausal hormone therapy, past users of the therapy, or never used it. The hormone therapy involved taking either estrogen alone, or in combination with progesterone and progestin.

The decade-long gain of fat mass and visceral adipose tissue seen in past users and never users did not show up in the current users of the hormone therapy. By staying on hormone therapy, those women effectively avoided most of the weight gain the other women experienced, especially tummy fat. However, when the users discontinued the use of hormone therapy, they began to gain weight again.

For women who completely lose their estrogen, visceral fat has been shown to increase by 10% in as little as five months. Needless to say, that's a lot! For other women, a gradual loss of estrogen contributes to a slowing of their body's metabolic rate, meaning they burn calories more slowly. Estrogen loss also causes fat cells around the abdomen to proliferate, disrupting sleep patterns and triggering more fat retention, while reducing energy levels which, of course, results in more sedentary behavior and more weight gain. It's another of those 'vicious cycles' that we seek to break with this self-healing diet book.

Salpeter SR. Et al. "Meta-analysis: effect of hormone-replacement therapy on components of the metabolic syndrome in postmenopausal women." Diabetes Obes Metab. 2006 September.
Dobs AS. Et al. "Differential Effects of Oral Estrogen versus Oral Estrogen-Androgen Replacement Therapy on Body Composition in Postmenopausal Women." J Clin Endocrinol Metab. 2002 April.
Papadakis GE. Et al. "Menopausal Hormone Therapy Is Associated With Reduced Total and Visceral Adiposity: The OsteoLaus Cohort." J Clin Endocrinol Metab. 2018 March.

When men gain weight, their level of testosterone in the body declines, whereas when they lose the weight, their testosterone rises again. Research has established this is why weight management is so important for having healthy testosterone when men enter middle age and beyond.

Related research has documented how drops in a man's testosterone production, as occurs with aging, also leads to weight gain, and once obesity sets in, that unhealthy condition further lowers testosterone production. If there was ever a 'vicious cycle' in life, this is it!

Losing testosterone produces weight gain, and that excess weight, in turn, depletes testosterone. It's no wonder so many men show evidence of 'Mano-Pause' - the male version of menopause in women - with all of its attendant symptoms of 'beer belly' and irritability and sleeplessness, and depression. (You may want to read our book on this subject, Mano-Pause, to learn more about how to counteract this condition.)

Testosterone replacement therapy (hormone therapy, for short) offers a proven antidote for men suffering from being overweight and the metabolic syndromes of diabetes, cardiovascular disease, etc. - which often accompany these mid-life bulges. This therapy appears safe for most men.

To illustrate our point, scientists with the *European Society of Endocrinology* did a study review in 2015, examining the results of 59 clinical trials of testosterone supplementation on body composition in men. They concluded: "Testosterone supplementation was associated with a significant reduction of fat and with an increase of lean mass."

As for the long-term effects of hormone therapy in men, study results are promising on that front as well. A group of 411 obese, hypogonadal men receiving injections of testosterone undecanoate at three-month intervals were studied over eight years by a team of scientists from Germany. The hormonal therapy was found to produce a "significant weight loss, decrease in waist circumference and body mass index." As the science team concluded, writing in the *International Journal of Obesity*, "Testosterone therapy appears to be an effective approach to achieve sustained weight loss in obese hypogonadal men irrespective of the severity of obesity. Based on these findings, we suggest that testosterone therapy offers safe and effective treatment of obesity."

Research out of the Boston University School of Medicine provides further support for the long-term weight loss benefits, without relapse, of this therapy. As reported in 2014: "Testosterone therapy

---

Camacho EM. Et al. "Age-associated changes in hypothalamic-pituitary-testicular function in middle-aged and older men are modified by weight change and lifestyle factors: longitudinal results from the European Male Ageing Study." Eur J Endocrinol. 2013 February.
Haider A. Et al. "Hypogonadal obese men with and without diabetes mellitus type 2 lose weight and show improvement in cardiovascular risk factors when treated with testosterone: an observational study." Obes Res Clin Pract. 2014 July-August.
Corona G. Et al. "Testosterone supplementation and body composition: results from a meta-analysis study." Eur Soc Endocrinol. 2015 November.

in obese men with testosterone deficiency represents a novel and timely therapeutic strategy for managing obesity in men. It produces sustained weight loss without recidivism."

Some older men will also find weight loss benefits in combining testosterone therapy with growth hormone supplementation. In a study of 122 overweight men, average age of 70 years, they were given transdermal testosterone plus growth hormone over 16 weeks and had their body composition regularly measured. The researchers at the Keck School of Medicine, University of Southern California, concluded: "Supplemental testosterone produced significant gains in total and appendicular lean mass, muscle strength, and aerobic endurance with significant reductions in whole-body and trunk fat. Outcomes appeared to be further enhanced with growth hormone supplementation."

Saad F. Et al. "Effects of long-term treatment with testosterone on weight and waist size in 411 hypogonadal men with obesity classes I-III: observational data from two registry studies." Int J Obes. 2016 January.
Traish AM. "Testosterone and weight loss: the evidence." Curr Opin Endocrinol Diabetes Obes. 2014 October.
Sattler FR. Et al. "Testosterone and growth hormone improve body composition and muscle performance in older men." J Clin Endocrinol Metab. 2009 June.

Body Fat Reduction with Freezing

Body invasive fat reduction procedures - bariatric surgery and liposuction, in particular - have been around for many years and generally are recommended only in cases of morbid obesity. The scientific evidence for short-term benefits and potential side effects is generally well-known. We want to focus on the evidence for two non-invasive techniques, *fat cell freezing* which have emerged as widely available options for initiating weight reduction.

Keep in mind that neither of these fat-reducing treatments we discuss in this section are long-term answers to keeping excess weight off, but since you may be tempted to try one, or more than one - or maybe you already have - we want you to have access to the latest scientific evidence about safety and effectiveness.

The first of these non-invasive procedures is called cryolipolysis (fat cell freezing), which has been popularized by such companies as CoolSculpting. Behind the technique is the idea that cold temperature exposure can help you trigger fat burning of what is known as brown fat tissue, the 'good fat' which helps us to burn off unhealthy and unsightly excess white fat that often accumulates on our thighs and around the midsection of our body.

When we are at our normal body temperatures, this brown fat is dormant. But when we are exposed to cold temperatures, brown fat burns - an estimated two ounces of it can release 500 calories a day - which happens as a result of shivering from the cold. Scientists believe this process is a survival mechanism programmed into us by evolution to help prevent hypothermia and freezing to death.

A study published in the science journal, *Cell Metabolism,* revealed in 2014, how shivering from the cold increases the circulation of two hormones in the body - FGF21 from brown fat and irisin, a hormone from muscle, both of which are also released during physical exercise. Activating these two hormones via cold temperatures, according to the study results, triggers the conversion of white fat cells into more beneficial brown fat cells, which results in a loss of body weight.

One way for you to experiment with this finding is to take cold showers or immerse yourself in cold water baths each day. Another application involves taking ritualistic cold-water plunges after being in a hot sauna. For many people this would be too slow of a fat-burning process, so the temptation is to use a faster-acting technique such as fat freezing.

Developed by two medical professors at Harvard University, cryolipolysis may be the most effective method available to destroy fat cells, but shouldn't be considered a complete substitute for healthy dieting and exercise. First approved for use in the U.S. by the Food and Drug Administration in 2010, the cryolipolysis device targets fat cells in specific body areas and freezes them away, without harming the surrounding skin.

The procedure involves reclining in a chair as a practitioner applies two cup-shaped panels to the skin of the treatment area. These panels release a painless combination of cooling temperature and a suction vacuum. Each session lasts less than an hour, swelling is minimal in the treated area and there is no wounding or residual discomfort. As for the crystallized and dead fat cells released by freezing, this waste is excreted by your body's lymphatic system for several months afterward.

Visible results from this process can be seen in about four weeks, and the fat reduction is often permanent unless you begin gaining weight again, which is what trips up many users. Science studies have examined the extent to which cryolipolysis is safe, painless, and effective. Therefore we would recommend it as a way to supplement the effects of healthy eating, dieting, and a daily exercise regime.

Lee P. Et al. "Irisin and FGF21 are cold-induced endocrine activators of brown fat function in humans." Cell Metab. 2014 February.

Among the findings from comprehensive reviews of the experimental evidence:

- Localized fat reduction was examined, in 2015, by the *Journal of Plastic & Reconstructive Surgery*, based on 19 studies of the technique. Average fat reduction ranged from 14.67 percent to 28.5 percent of body weight and came with only mild, short-term side effects.

- Scientists writing in the *Journal of Aesthetic Surgery* reviewed the medical literature in 2015, assessing 16 studies that followed 1,445 patients. "The mean reduction of subcutaneous tissue was 19.5 percent," over an evaluation period of almost four months, concluded the reviewers, and complications were found to be uncommon.

- A 2018 study in the *Journal of Cosmetic Dermatology* evaluated four clinical trials of 101 persons: "There was a statistically significant reduction in fat and while patients expressed high satisfaction with the treatment," wrote the study review co-authors, "and adverse effects were mild and transient."

After the U.S. Food and Drug Administration approved cryolipolysis for fat reduction of the abdomen, scientists also began to study whether this nonsurgical technique could be effective for *fat reduction of the thighs*. For example, University of Minnesota Medical School scientists did a thigh reduction study in 2015, with 45 test subjects who received 60 minutes of cryolipolysis treatments, followed by two minutes of manual massage. The study participants did follow-up visits at 8 and 16 weeks, and ultrasound and other measurements were taken to determine the average inner thigh fat reduction. Fat layer reductions averaged 2.8 mm. When study participants filled out questionnaires about their experiences, 84 percent claimed significant fat reduction.

Scientists from the University of California at Davis School of Medicine, and the University of Minnesota Medical School, studied 60 persons who had visible second chin skin flaps. Each was given a single treatment cycle, at -10 degrees Celsius for 60 minutes. A second optional treatment was delivered 6 weeks later. At study's end, 77 percent reported visible fat reduction and felt their appearance improved, and none had adverse side effects.

Ingargiola MJ. Et al. "Cryolipolysis for fat reduction and body contouring: safety and efficacy of current treatment paradigms." Plast Recostru Surg. 2015 June.
Derrick CD. Et al. "The Safety and Efficacy of Cryolipolysis: A Systematic Review of Available Literature." Aesthet Surg J. 2015 September.
Lipner SR. "Cryolipolysis for the treatment of submental fat: Review of the literature." J Cosmet Dermatol. 2018 January.
Zelickson BD. Et al. "Cryolipolysis for safe and effective inner thigh fat reduction." Lasers Surg Med. 2015 February.
Kilmer SL. Et al. "Safety and efficacy of cryolipolysis for non-invasive reduction of submental fat." Lasers Surg Med. 2016 January.

Loose skin under the arms can be unsightly and difficult to get rid of. Scientists at the University of British Columbia tested in 2017, whether cryolipolysis could be an effective fat reducer in that part of the body, using 30 female test subjects. Both arms of each participant received 35 minutes of treatment of cryolipolysis at -11 degrees Celsius. Fat reduction measurements were taken at 1, 4, and 12 weeks, post-treatment, and the average fat reduction in both arms was found to be 3.2 mm, without adverse side effects.

Scientists at the University of Pennsylvania, School of Medicine, examined cryolipolysis to selectively destroy fat cells in the neck by testing 12 women and two men whose average age was 50 years. After two 45-minute sessions, with a 6-week follow-up, an average fat layer reduction of 2.3 mm in the neck of participants was found. "The study demonstrates," wrote the study authors, "that cryolipolysis is well tolerated and produces visible and significant fat layer reduction."

To reiterate, fat freezing shouldn't be treated as a panacea for weight loss, it's more in the category of a jumpstarting supplemental procedure to assist regular exercise and a consistently healthy diet in keeping the pounds off in the long term.

Carruthers JD. Et al. "Cryolipolysis for Reduction of Arm Fat: Safety and Efficacy of a Prototype CoolCup Applicator With Fat Contour." Dematol Surgery. 2017 July.
Bernstein EF. Et al. "Safety and Efficacy of Bilateral Submental Cryolipolysis With Quantified 3-Dimensional Imaging of Fat Reduction and Skin Tightening." JAMA Facial Plast Surg. 2017 September.

Regular Cold Exposure Can Help Burn Fat

There is evidence that people living in colder climates are generally less overweight and certainly less obese than persons living in warmer climates, and scientific research provides us with an answer - regular exposure to coldness helps to burn body fat by speeding up the body's metabolism and activating brown fat.

One of the pioneers in researching this weight loss angle is a biologist at the Netherlands Maastricht University, Wouter van Marken Lichtenbelt, whose series of studies over the past decade focused on how temperature variances indoors influence human health in general, and in particular, body weight. Consider the results from one of his studies in 2013, using 17 people in their early 20's.

For 10 days, these volunteers spent an increasing amount of time in a room where the thermostat was set at 59 degrees Fahrenheit. By the end of the 10-day period, they were spending six hours a day in the room. By day 10, their metabolism sped up and they were burning 30 percent more calories than before the experiment began. They were burning their body's store of brown fat in response to the chilly temperature.

"We should not assume comfortable is always healthy," explained Lichtenbelt, assessing the findings. "Sometimes you have to get out of your comfort zone."

Van der Lans AA. Et al. "Cold acclimation recruits human brown fat and increases nonshivering thermogenesis." J Clin Invest. 2013 August.

As he and his colleagues further explained in one of their studies, "variable indoor environments with frequent cold exposures might be an acceptable and economic manner to increase energy expenditure and may contribute to counteracting the current obesity epidemic."

These study results have been affirmed by Japanese scientists, who found drops of four pounds of body fat over six weeks from two hours a day spent in 63 degrees temperatures. A group of these scientists declared in 2015, in the science journal, *Annals of Medicine*: "Human brown adipose tissue is activated by acute cold exposure, being positively correlated by cold-induced increases in energy expenditure. The inverse relationship between the brown adipose tissue activity and body fatness suggests that brown adipose tissue, because of its energy-dissipating activity, is protective against body fat accumulation."

Given these study results and conclusions, we may infer not only should you keep temperatures indoors cooler than you normally do, but there will also be heightened weight loss benefits to you if you exercise vigorously outside, in cold weather, to further activate your metabolism and fat burning.

Vijgen GH. Et al. "Vagus nerve stimulation increases energy expenditure: relation to brown adipose tissue activity." PLoS One. 2013 October.
Yoneshiro T. Saito M. "Activation and recruitment of brown adipose tissue as anti-obesity regimens in humans." Ann Med. 2015 March.

Saunas Can Melt Away Pounds

Among wrestlers and judo competitors preparing for the Olympics, it's well-known that some will significantly and rapidly reduce their body weight in the days before a match by using steam saunas. This can help them stay within their weight class to qualify for a match and may even give them a competitive advantage against opponents.

Though we do not recommend using saunas solely for rapid weight loss, there are long- term weight and overall health benefits by doing so. Unlike conventional saunas that make you perspire to relax, Far Infrared Saunas use infrared heaters that release infrared light and a radiant penetrating heat, which your skin absorbs enabling you to release toxins from body fat. The infrared effect penetrates several inches into the skin, far deeper in its effects than you experience with conventional saunas.

Science evidence indicates that infrared penetration can improve cardiovascular and heart function, making it useful in treating hypertension. Japanese scientists have found this thermal treatment, called Waon therapy in Japan, to be effective in treating fibromyalgia and other forms of pain, as well as cardiovascular disease.

The advantage of using Far Infrared saunas in detoxifying the body of chemicals and heavy metals is that you release some of the obesogens (as we discuss earlier in this book) which may be contributing to your weight gain and your inability to lose weight in the long term. So, adding regular sauna sessions, whether conventional dry or wet saunas, or Far Infrared, can assist you in achieving your weight loss goals, particularly if you add resistance training or aerobic exercise before your sauna sessions.

Artioli GG. Et al. "Prevalence, Magnitude, and Methods of Rapid Weight Loss among Judo Competitors." Medicine & Science in Sports & Exercise. 2009.
Matsushita K. Et al. "Efficacy of Waon Therapy for Fibromyalgia." Internal Medicine. 2008.

Yet another temperature-related fat-fighting tool you could consider might be *hot tubs or just hot baths,* with Epsom salts added, or the natural detoxifier, magnesium, (you can also use magnesium flakes) that can help flush toxins out of the body.

Study evidence evaluating the effects of *saunas and hot tubs* indicates these treatments exert health benefits to the body, similar to the effects that exercise training produces, and can release pounds of fat if you spend 30 minutes a day, six days a week, immersed in hot water. Hot bathing increases the circulation of free fatty acids, a process helpful for reducing insulin resistance, triggering the body to break up fat deposits, a process called lipolysis.

As one study of regular thermal therapy exposure concluded: "For those who lack ready access to a sauna or communal hot tub, regular hot baths at home may suffice as practical thermal therapy {which} might be viewed as an alternative to exercise training in patients too physically impaired for significant aerobic activity."

McCarty MF. Et al. "Regular thermal therapy may promote insulin sensitivity while boosting expression of endothelial nitric oxide synthase—effects comparable to those of exercise training." Med Hypotheses. 2009 July. Also, Pall ML. "Do sauna therapy and exercise act by raising the availability of tetrahydrobiopterin?" Med Hypotheses. 2009 October.

Lose Weight While You Sleep

Sounds too good to be true, doesn't it!? But in this instance, it's NOT trickery. Scientific evidence shows that depending on when you take a 'power nap' and how long you sleep can help you to lose weight. (As you may recall from earlier in this book, sleeping too much or too little can contribute to gaining weight; in this case, when you nap and for how long, can help to counteract the negative impacts of too little or too much overall sleep.)

Scientists writing in the journal, *Current Biology,* tested the idea that energy expenditure (burning calories) is affected by the times you choose to sleep as well as the length of sleep, all of which affect the circadian rhythm system of the human body, the 24-hour cycle that runs the body's internal clock.

What the study found was that test subjects monitored during short afternoon naps had a much higher resting energy expenditure than at other times of the day. An estimated 10% more calories were burned by the body while sleeping during afternoons compared to other sleep cycles.

These findings may contribute to an understanding of why shift workers and others with irregular sleep schedules have a tendency to gain more weight than people with regular sleep patterns. It is information that also underscores the weight loss potential for 'power napping' during early afternoons.

Zitting KM. Et al. "Human Resting Energy Expenditure Varies with Circadian Phase." Curr Biology. 2018 November 19.

How Many Daily Steps Do You Need?

For the first time, in 2022, a science-based finding emerged of how many steps you should walk each day to either maintain your current weight, or to lose unwanted pounds. As an added bonus, we also learned how many daily steps will help to protect you from diabetes, sleep apnea, acid reflux, and depression.

A team of 12 scientists monitored 6,042 test subjects over four years, tracking the number of steps they took daily as recorded by wearable Fitbit devices. The test subjects were 73% women, ranging in age from 41 to 67 years, and their body mass index ranged from 24.3 (a healthy weight range) to 32 and above (obese.) During the four years of walk monitoring, their incidence of disease was also recorded.

Those who walked around 8,200 steps per day (about four miles) were not only less likely to become overweight, they were less likely to develop depression, acid reflux, and sleep apnea, as well as diabetes. For those who were already overweight, increasing their step counts to 11,000 a day resulted in a 50% increase in their protection against obesity. Even more health benefits occurred for people who walked at a brisk pace of 112 steps a minute, for up to 30 minutes.

Whether you decide to use a wearable step-tracking device or not, to record your progress, you might consider incorporating more steps into your daily routine as a lifestyle choice. One way is to make a habit of walking on a treadmill while watching all of your favorite television shows and movies. If you don't have a treadmill, set aside an hour to take brisk walks, preferably in Nature, while counting your steps or listening to some inspiring music, or both!

Master H. Et al. "Association of step counts over time with the risk of chronic disease in the All of Us Research Program." Nature Medicine. 2022.

When You Exercise Does Matter

If you are like most people, you never stop thinking about which time of day for exercise is most conducive to losing weight. Not even fitness coaches pay much attention to the timing of workouts, but timing does matter because men and women possess different circadian rhythms for burning calories.

This fact emerged from a 2022 study, in New York, in which 30 women and 26 men were randomly placed into two exercise groups—one group did 12 weeks of training in the mornings, one group did 12 weeks of workouts in the evenings. During the study period everyone had their abdominal fat and body composition measured periodically, along with their muscular strength and endurance.

What surfaced after 12 weeks was clear evidence that morning exercise reduced abdominal fat in women, whereas evening exercise enhanced their muscular performance. For men, it was different: by exercising in the evening, the men burned more fat than in the morning and also lowered their blood pressure.

These results provide one more factor for you to take into account when choosing the timing of an exercise routine to help you lose weight.

Arciero PJ. Et al. "Morning Exercise Reduces Abdominal Fat and Blood Pressure in Women; Evening Exercise Increases Muscular Performance in Women and Lowers Blood Pressure in Men." Front Physiology. 2022 May 31.

Action Tip: Feeling Good Vibrations

For people who are physically unable to engage in vigorous exercise to lose weight, an option exists that could 'vibrate away' some of the unwanted fat.

It's called whole-body vibration and involves standing, sitting or lying on a vibrating platform that transmits energy into the body, prompting muscles to contract and relax dozens of times every second. By doing it 15 minutes a day, for three or more days of the week, initial scientific evidence shows that the process helps with weight loss while improving muscle strength, reducing bone loss and protecting against falls among people of all ages, but most especially the elderly. It has become popular in health and fitness centers as a training tool.

Chinese scientists did an animal study for eight weeks using whole-body vibration, while monitoring the effects on weight, metabolism, and blood markers. They discovered the technique promotes brown-fat-like changes in white adipose (fat) tissues to an extent similar to what exercise normally induces. As they related in the science journal, Biomedical Research International, not only can the vibration turn bad (white) fat into good (brown) fat, it stimulates the secretion of growth hormone and testosterone, while is also helpful in fat reduction.

Italian scientists conducted a vibration training study with 50 obese women, average age of 46 years, over a ten-week period that involved two sessions a week. The women were divided up into a control group who made no lifestyle changes, and an intervention group who did the weekly vibration training that included arm and leg exercises.

At the end of 10 weeks, the vibration group showed "significantly lower body mass index, total body and trunk fat," the science team reported, as well as improved muscular strength.

How this occurs was described by the science team as the radiofrequency effects of a rapid oscillating vibrating platform increasing oxygen consumption and inducing muscular contractions in the human body, similar to what happens with exercise.

More research and longer clinical trials remain to be done, but these preliminary effects make whole-body vibration seem to be a useful and safe complementary technique when paired with healthy eating and exercise routines.

Sun C. Et al. "Vibration Training Triggers Brown Adipocyte Relative Protein Expression in Rat White Adipose Tissue." Biomed Res Int. 2015.
Milanese C. Et al. "Ten-week Whole-body Vibration Training Improves Body Composition and Muscle Strength in Obese Women." Int J Med Sci. 2013.

Some other lower-cost and more rudimentary options you might try to get some similar benefits are:

Jumping rope. If you are physically able, jumping rope enables you to not only vibrate your body with every jump, but to burn calories as you do.

Jumping on a trampoline. Like rope jumping, you vibrate your body while burning calories, though not nearly as many calories burned as with jump ropes.

(Be sure to check with your physician if you have any injuries or concerns before attempting these exercises.)

Action Tip: 'Power Naps' to Burn Calories

Take a 10-minute, but no more than 30-minute, 'power nap' to recharge your alertness and burn some calories. Anything more than 30 minutes may leave you feeling drowsy and unable to focus when you wake up.

1. Choose a time in the early or mid-afternoon.

2. Have a dark and quiet space for you to lay down.

3. Set an alarm clock for 10 to 30 minutes. Get up immediately, don't linger in bed.

"Should You Take Power Naps?" Cleveland Clinic. November 22, 2021. www.health.clevelandclinic.org/power-naps/

Action Tip: Burn Fat by Exercising Before Breakfast

There have been two traditional points of view about the timing of exercise around breakfast. One holds that eating first in the morning, before you exercise, results in a blood sugar boost that helps with the length and intensity of working out, without increasing weight. The other perspective holds that you will burn more calories and thus, more fat, if you exercise and then eat your normal breakfast.

Scientific evidence has been accumulating over the past few years that the latter approach may hold more weight loss potential for many people than the other perspective. Two studies done in Britain, at the University of Bath and three other universities, put the two approaches to the test in a series of trials involving groups of healthy young men and obese or overweight men.

In the 2019 study, using blood testing and other physiological measures, the scientists saw how exercising without food (fuel) in the body forces it to burn stored carbohydrates and then, when those are burned, to begin depleting reserves of fat cells. Their findings contributed to the idea that a negative daily energy balance - that is, skipping breakfast before exercise - can be a useful strategy for long-term weight gain prevention.

A similar study done two years earlier, involving many of the same research team, also using blood samples collected at regular intervals among test subjects, found adipose tissue gene expression is affected by exercise before eating and "these acute exercise-induced changes could be part of the mechanism through which exercise improves health."

Edinburgh RM. Et al. "Skipping Breakfast Before Exercise Creates a More Negative 24-hour Energy Balance: A Randomized Controlled Trial in Healthy Physically Active Young Men." J Nutr. 2019 August.
Chen YC. Et al. "Feeding influences adipose tissue responses to exercise in overweight men." Am J Physiol Endocrinol Metab. 2017 March.

Lifestyle Rituals for Weight Health

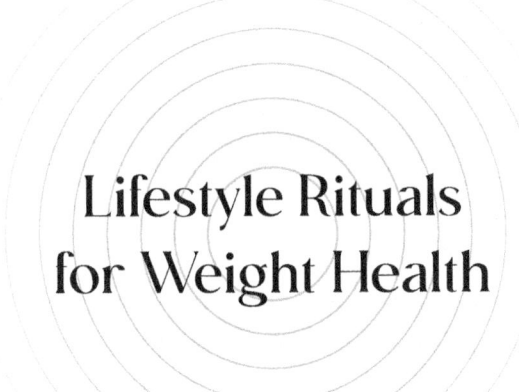

Combine Healthy Habits to Amplify Effects

We have written extensively in past books about the concept of synergy, how the impact of any one factor can be magnified when combined with two or more other factors. This interaction concept holds true for both the negative health effects of toxins, as well as the health-supportive effects of healing nutrients acting together.

Why wouldn't this same concept apply to losing weight? We believe that it does!

As we discussed in Part 2, we know that weight loss programs fail for a variety of reasons, not the least of which is they address too few supportive factors in a person's life that influences their chances for long-term success. Study evidence affirms that combined approaches to losing weight are more effective than single approaches, such as what happens when you just follow the directions in a fad diet. To illustrate what we mean, scientists writing in the *British Journal of Nutrition* found that adding cognitive behavioral treatment (which helps address underlying behaviors contributing to weight gain) combined with a low-fat or low- carbohydrate diet "produced significantly greater short-term weight loss in obese women compared with diet alone."

In this section of our book, we tackle what you need to do so you lose weight steadily and safely, but slow enough so that your loss of weight doesn't set off so many alarms in your brain that it becomes your own worst enemy in achieving your weight loss goals.

Rodriguez-Hernandez H. Et al. "Adding cognitive behavioral treatment to either low-carbohydrate or low-fat diets: differential short-term effects." Br J Nutr. 2009 December.

You will learn how to train yourself to prefer and choose healthy foods, along with how to summon the willpower to maintain your dietary plan. That behavioral change component offers proven ways to help counteract the important but under-recognized roles that pessimism, self-loathing, and self-sabotage play in undermining weight loss goals.

We spotlight science-backed techniques and concepts for you to integrate into your life for healthy weight maintenance and to create a positive lifestyle synergy. We also describe a range of specific foods and supplements to satisfy food cravings and trigger natural body mechanisms to keep off excess pounds.

> The most credible and sustainable weight loss and weight maintenance results come when people stick to a complete system combining science-proven techniques that personalize their individual needs.

Make Exercise a Lifestyle Choice

You can't just rely on exercise alone to reduce fat and keep it off you! Regular vigorous physical activity is one of the pillars that helps accomplish weight management goals, but it isn't a panacea for success if the other necessary elements of a lifestyle program aren't in place, particularly a proper diet. You can't put nutrient-poor food into your body and expect it to perform optimally, no matter how regularly or vigorously you exercise, any more than you can pump low-quality fuel into your car engine and expect to win a race.

Exercise is more important to your overall health and for disease prevention than it is for achieving weight loss, especially if you continue eating a toxic diet. Experts in kinesiology from three U.S. universities investigated this angle in 2018, when they assessed the scientific literature and concluded, "although the minimum guidelines for aerobic physical activity (150 minutes of moderate or 75 minutes of vigorous physical activity per week) can improve cardiovascular health, these levels are generally inadequate for clinically significant weight loss or weight maintenance without caloric restriction."

A huge amount of scientific research has been done on which specific exercises will burn the most calories. For our purposes, in this book, we won't sort through that mass of material except to give you a few examples of low-impact forms of exercise you might be able to incorporate easily into your daily routine.

Swift DL. Et al. "The Effects of Exercise and Physical Activity on Weight Loss and Maintenance." Prog Cardiovasc Dis. 2018 July-August.

Doing a daily fast walk, combined with a low-calorie diet, can bring you gradual but steady benefits in losing and maintaining weight, with much less risk of physical injury as might occur from aerobics or high-intensity training. Scientists in Italy, in 2019, tested normal walking versus Nordic walking to evaluate which can have the greatest benefit for weight and body composition.

Nordic walking involves walking in long strides with a lightweight pole in each hand, swinging the arms, much like a cross-country skier. The arm movement with the poles builds muscle in the arms and further raises the walking heart rate and energy expenditure. In a test of this exercise among 38 overweight people, it was compared to a control group who walked the same distances and at the same speed but without the poles. Both groups ate similar healthy diets.

At the end of six months, the Nordic walkers had decreased their body mass index by 6%, compared to 4% for the normal walkers, but the Nordic walkers had also reduced total body fat by 8% and leg fat by 9%, whereas the normal walkers showed no significant change. Another Nordic advantage was the dropout rate was 21% compared to 36% in the normal walking group, indicating that the Nordic routine kept people's interest longer. These findings prompted the science team to declare: "Nordic walking provides greater and faster benefits than walking and thus can be a primary tool to counteract the obesity and overweight state in middle-aged adults."

It's important to note that walking briskly for 15 minutes after a large meal not only assists the body with digestion and nutrient absorption, and helps to balance blood sugar levels; by speeding up digestion with a walk, you are less likely to absorb the food you eat as fat. That should give you better weight loss results. (While you are walking, it also helps to take long strides and swing your arms, especially while walking uphill, which will further accelerate burning calories and fat.)

A second popular low-impact form of exercise that produces weight loss is having a yoga practice. Many people just assume that a stretching exercise provides few, if any, benefits to weight maintenance. Science studies have disproven this assumption.

Muollo V. Et al. "The effects of exercise and diet program in overweight people—Nordic walking versus walking." Clin Interv Aging. 2019 August.

Here are a few examples:

- A study involving 15,550 adults, aged 53 to 57 years, tracking their weight over a 10-year period, found that participants who began the study while overweight and doing yoga (one 30-minute session per week) ended up losing five to 18 pounds while those persons who didn't have a yoga practice gained an average of 14 pounds.

- In a 2017 study of 1,830 young adults, it was discovered that the frequency of their yoga practice produced more weight loss over time, particularly in those who were overweight, prompting the scientists to conclude: "Practicing yoga on a regular basis may help with weight gain prevention."

- The medical journal, *Preventive Medicine*, published a comparative review of 30 clinical trials of yoga for weight loss, involving 2,173 participants, and concluded from the evidence that yoga can be "considered a safe and effective intervention to reduce body mass index in overweight or obese individuals."

Whichever exercise routine you choose, make sure you are consistent about it. Even if you believe you are being consistent in your commitment, this question may arise for you: Why do I fail to lose weight over the long term despite maintaining a regular intense workout routine? The answer may be that you are unknowingly engaged in self-sabotaging behaviors.

Kristal AR. Et al. "Yoga practice is associated with attenuated weight gain in healthy, middle-aged men and women." Altern Ther Health Med. 2005 July-August. Neumark-Sztainer D. Et al. "How Is the Practice of Yoga Related to Weight Status? Population-Based Findings From Project EAT-IV." J Phys Act Health. 2017 December. Lauche R. Et al. "A systematic review and meta-analysis on the effects of yoga on weight-related outcomes." Prev Med. 2016 June.

Beware of Sabotaging Behaviors

Compensatory behaviors are unconscious adjustments most people make after exercise that end up offsetting the benefits of the calories burned by exercise.

For example, after a workout, you 'reward' yourself by taking it easy for the rest of the day, lounging on a couch, watching television and, in the process, lowering your normal metabolic rate. Or you 'reward' yourself by having a second dessert after dinner, and before you know it, that has become a ritual.

Scientists at the University of Colorado, School of Medicine, studied this phenomenon of compensatory behaviors in 2013, finding that "some individuals adopt compensatory behaviors, that is, increased energy intake and/or reduced activity, that offset the exercise energy expenditure and limit weight loss." Many people engaging in this undermining of weight loss goals have no awareness of these self-sabotaging behaviors, or else they have rationalized away their behaviors as having limited or no impact on weight loss.

There is also the physiological and psychological phenomenon of predicted and expected weight loss versus the actual weight that is lost from various exercise regimens. Scientists have formulated how many calories should be burned and, thus, how much weight should be lost from specific exercises, such as walking versus running versus swimming. They even have formulas for the amount of time that needs to be spent at various exertion levels in order to maintain weight loss.

Melanson EL. Et al. "Resistance to exercise-induced weight loss: compensatory behavioral adaptations." Med Sci Sports Exerc. 2013 August.

But all of the formulas are subject to alteration by a wildcard factor of 'compensatory responses' by exercisers, which involves unconscious body responses that compensate for energy expended in exercise, to the unconscious mental compensations that involve behaviors. To illustrate, exercise physiologists from three U.S. universities conducted a study with 94 overweight or obese postmenopausal women to test their responses to either 72, 136, or 194 minutes of training exercises each week.

Over six months, the women in the three exercise time groups did their workout routines to achieve a heart rate associated with 50% of their peak heart rate. Weight loss was predicted for each group based on calories burned multiplied by the minutes of exercise performed each week.

At the study's conclusion, women exercising for the longest each week, 194 minutes, only achieved half of their predicted weight loss. In other words, with longer durations of exercise, this group of women became what the scientists called 'compensators' as a result of their bodies and minds resisting and compensating for the energy expended. Weight loss was more predictable and sustainable for the two groups of women exercising at 72 and 136 minutes a week, prompting the science team to observe "exercise in promoting weight loss is far more complicated than expected."

Taken together, all of these scientific findings bring us back to the importance of having a behavioral change component in place when you create a weight management plan.

For the relative calorie-burning benefits of various forms of exercise, the Centers for Disease Control and Prevention distilled the scientific evidence and posted this chart on its website: www.cdc.gov/healthyweight/physical_activity

Church TS. Et al. "Changes in Weight, Waist Circumference and Compensatory Responses with Different Doses of Exercise among Sedentary, Overweight Postmenopausal Women." PLoS One. 2009.

Create Your Own Weight Management Plan

Have you ever thought of having your own personalized weight maintenance program to integrate into your daily life? It's worth considering because the scientific evidence shows that combining multiple elements of weight loss approaches and techniques produces much more powerful and longer-lasting results than just relying on diet and exercise alone.

As the opening sentence of a study published in the science journal, *Eating & Weight Disorders,* framed the challenge most overweight people face: "The overarching problem in the treatment of obesity is the consistency with which weight {in treatment} is regained."

In 2018, scientists from South Korea tested the effects of combining exercise with alternate- day calorie restriction, versus exercise alone or calorie restriction alone. They divided 45 overweight or obese adults, aged 32 to 40 years of age, into four groups: a control group, an exercise-only group, a calorie restriction-only group, and a group using exercise and calorie restriction together. The study lasted eight weeks and the exercise portion involved both resistance training and aerobics classes.

Of the four groups contrasted, the researchers found that "the combined intervention {of exercise plus calorie restriction} was most effective in inducing beneficial changes in body weight and body composition."

In another test of a multi-factor approach for treatment, 50 obese patients, each of whom had previously lost 10% of their weight using a dieting program, were placed on a weight maintenance plan that involved cognitive behavioral therapy, a diet program, physical activity, counseling, and

Oh M. Et al. "Effects of alternate day calorie restriction and exercise on cardio-metabolic risk factors in overweight and obese adults: an exploratory randomized controlled study." BMC Public Health. 2018 September.

an on-and-off prescription of orlistat over a two-year period. By study's end, 90% of the participants had maintained their more than 10% weight loss, demonstrating that by combining a variety of factors into a cohesive program over time, promising results occur in keeping lost weight off. As the researchers acknowledged, the key is to create individualized plans to make these long-term maintenance plans even more effective.

Other studies of multi-faceted weight plans found similar promising results, particularly when cognitive therapy was added to other treatments to prevent relapse and weight regain. In 2009, for example, a study divided 204 persons who were overweight or obese into two groups: one received dietary treatment plus cognitive therapy, the other group got dietary treatment and physical exercise. After the study ended, "participants in the cognitive dietetic treatment maintained all their weight loss, whereas participants in the physical exercise dietetic treatment regained part (25%) of their lost weight," reported the researchers.

Swiss scientists conducted a study in which 61 weight-challenged patients with a binge eating disorder were divided into three groups: a purely cognitive behavioral therapy (CBT) treatment, or a CBT combined with a nutritional approach to restrict fat intake, or a CBT combined with both a nutritional and physical activity approach. The experiment lasted for 12 weeks. At the end of that time, it was the third group combining CBT with the nutritional and physical exercise treatments which had, by far, the most significant positive effects, including decreased "negative mood, improved eating disorders and leading to an effective body weight loss," wrote the research team.

The importance of peer group bonding and group support during physical activities, in reaching weight loss goals, was apparent in the results of a study published in the *International Journal of Obesity*. A group of 76 overweight adolescents, aged 13 to 16 years, were recruited as study participants. They were assigned to one of two treatment groups: cognitive behavioral treatment combined with 'adventure therapy' similar to the group physical activities of Outward Bound, or a cognitive behavioral group combined with aerobic exercise. While the kids in both treatment groups lost "significant weight" over the 16 weeks of intervention, more kids in the CBT plus adventure therapy maintained a minimum of 10 pounds of weight loss at the end of treatment and beyond. The bonding and support from extended periods of outdoor physical activities had more long-term effects than being involved in an aerobics class.

Makoundou V. Et al. "A 2-year multifactor approach of weight loss maintenance." Eat Weight Disord. 2010 March.
Werrij MQ. Et al. "Adding cognitive therapy to dietetic treatment is associated with loss relapse in obesity." J Psychosom Res. 2009 October.
Fossati M. Et al. "Cognitive-behavioral therapy with simultaneous nutritional and physical activity education in obese patients with binge eating disorder." Eat Weight Disord. 2004 June.

A 2008 survey of the scientific literature on weight loss uncovered this finding: when cognitive behavioral therapy is added to low-calorie diet therapies in studies, an additional 11 pounds of weight loss, on average, occurs over a two-year period; the further addition of regular exercise to this mix produces another 2 to 3 pounds of weight loss over the same period.

What happens when you merge cognitive behavioral therapy with adherence to a Mediterranean diet in treating obesity? That was the question medical researchers at the University of Murcia, Spain, asked and answered in the journal, *Nutrition.* Working with 1,406 obese people aged 20 to 65 years, the researchers measured their body composition over 34 weeks as they kept on the behavioral therapy program while eating the Mediterranean diet. The average weight loss was more than 15 pounds, and just as impressively, the dropout rate was less than 9% of the participants.

The Hippocrates Self-Healing Diet contains significantly higher amounts of weight- reducing benefits than the more commonly referenced Mediterranean Diet.

Scientists at Maastricht University in The Netherlands, also examined the dropout rate in a program with and without cognitive behavioral therapy, in their study of 204 overweight and obese adults. Half of the group combined a low-calorie diet with cognitive therapy, while the other half combined a dietary treatment with a physical exercise regimen. Both treatments resulted in "significant decreases" in body mass index, the scientists reported, but "in the long run the cognitive dietetic treatment maintained all their weight loss, whereas participants in the physical exercise dietetic treatment regained part (25%) of their lost weight."

What this research indicates is how important creating your own weight management plan is achieving sustainable purging of the pounds.

Jelalian E. Et al. "Adventure therapy combined with cognitive-behavioral treatment for overweight adolescents." Int J Obes. 2006 January.
Clifton PM. "Dietary treatment for obesity." Nat Clin Pract Gastroenterol Hepatol. 2008 December.
Carbalan MD. Et al. "Effectiveness of cognitive-behavioral therapy based on the Mediterranean diet for the treatment of obesity." Nutrition. 2009 July-August.
Werrij MQ. Et al. "Adding cognitive therapy to dietetic treatment is associated with less relapse in obesity." J Psychosom Res. 2009 October.

To create your weight management lifestyle plan, ideally, you should choose some or all of these key components:

- routinely eat a plant-based diet (If you're worried about getting enough protein in your diet, put your mind at ease, you can get all the protein you need from beans, lentils, peas, peanuts, pistachios, chia and hemp seeds, tempeh and tofu, and even spinach.)

- have a daily exercise routine lasting at least 20 minutes

- do a daily meditation to help reduce stress and induce good sleep

- visualize your goal every day

- detoxify yourself of toxins with far-infrared and steam saunas

- use cognitive therapy to reinforce your goal commitments

- master skill-power techniques to reduce food cravings and bolster self-control.

Our Hippocrates Self-Healing Diet Program

It's no secret that the Hippocrates Wellness weight loss diet that we offer guests at our West Palm Beach, Florida, health resort, is the highest in protein, minerals, vitamins, and phytochemicals of any diet ever conceived.

Our state-of-the-art fitness component includes circuit and resistance training along with stretching exercises in a group setting, creating comradery as well as motivation. Just as important as exercising our body is exercising our mind. We believe that cultivating a healthy mindset is essential to creating and achieving personal health goals, and that involves visualizing yourself every day at your ideal weight. Having a healthy mindset starts with nurturing self-love. By practicing self-love in the form of compassion for yourself and others, and doing so on a daily basis, you will make losing weight inevitable. Healthy eating is a self-love practice, and so is regular exercise.

Ninety percent of the body's serotonin - a mood-stabilizing and appetite-controlling hormone - comes from the (GI) intestinal tract, which means you must have a balanced flora. Once we eliminate the propellers of fermentation in the GI, like sugars and complex carbohydrates, the fuel to lower serotonin and harm the immune system is no longer present. Then we give you a high plant protein diet to satiate you and regulate the sugars, so your brain is working with your bloodstream to regulate appetite and hunger.

The essential fats are the energy source for human cells. A 200-pound man can get all the glucose he needs daily from two medium-sized salads. When you get dependent on fuel from essential healthy fats, such as from avocado and chia seeds, versus a dependency on sugar, you burn more calories and lose more weight. Essential fatty acids only come from plants. To burn white fat off, you need to make brown fat from exercise and good sleep, all of which we emphasize and teach in our program.

As described by our professional exercise physiologists, another big reason why our methodical approach is effective and so highly recommended: "If you lose weight too quickly using impulsive, drastic non-scientific measures, your body can go into shock, and then the pounds actually come back even faster - and sometimes double the yo-yo effect. In addition, your skin does not have enough time to catch up to the rest of your body, resulting in loose skin."

Action Tip: Our Program Guidelines for Healthy Weight

We meet the human body's nutritional needs by using 80% living and raw food and 20% cooked (in a proper way) food, with a sensible balance and appropriate amounts.

One key 'secret weapon' component of our dietary program, missing from most if not all weight loss regimens, utilizes wheat grass juice, which contains a wealth of vitamins and minerals necessary for cell repair, including zinc, magnesium, calcium, and vitamins B, A, C, and E. It also creates a body environment that assists in purging ingested toxins and suppressing toxic bacterial growth, all of which facilitates the weight loss process.

You don't need to be 'gluten-intolerant' to get benefits from eliminating gluten from your diet. You will also get a fat loss effect by cutting gluten out of your life, which our diet accomplishes.

Aside from our nutrient-dense diet being unprocessed, organic, and GMO-free, it contains no caffeine, table salt, processed sugar, dairy, any animal foods (and that includes fish and eggs), and no artificial chemicals, alcohol, or preservatives.

We have accumulated many dozens of testimonials from Hippocrates visitors from throughout the world, who used our program, with great success, to lose countless pounds and keep them off. On our website, you will find these videos and much more, explaining our unique and proven approach to health.

For more on our weight management program, The Hippocrates Weight Loss/Fitness Academy, go to: www.hippocrateswellness.org/hwla.

Your Diet Choices Carry Climate Consequences

Choosing from among the many weight loss options can bring you directly into either alignment - or into conflict - with the global initiatives underway to slow global warming and protect planetary life. With dieting, you really do face a stark choice, continue to contribute to the problem or be a part of the larger solution. Exercising your choice and, with it, your responsibility to yourself and the planet begins with whether you select a plant-based diet to shed weight or stick with a diet containing meat and dairy products.

It's now common knowledge that red meat consumption increases your risk of heart disease, stroke, cancer, and type 2 diabetes. A plant-based diet avoids these health risks. But the scientific evidence also now proves that animal agriculture contributes in significant ways to the acceleration of climate change and the deterioration of our environment.

Three greenhouse gases - carbon dioxide, methane, and nitrous oxide - make the largest contribution to the temperature rises we humans have experienced over the past 100 years, a period that has been the warmest in recorded history. Carbon Footprint is the term applied to the sum total of gases (greenhouse emissions) from any human activity that sends emissions into the atmosphere, warming up the planet.

As noted elsewhere in this book, micronutrient deficiencies in our food crops continue to intensify as a result of climate change, particularly as a consequence of carbon dioxide emissions that alter nutrient formation in soils. The cycle of weight gain seen in most countries over the past half-century mirrors the cycle of mineral depletion from soils documented over the same period.

_{"Climate Change." United States Department of Agriculture, Economic Research Service. https://www.ers.usda.gov/topics/natural-resources-environment/climate-change/}

The five nutrients considered most essential for maintaining the health of your metabolism - B vitamins, Vitamin D, Iron, Calcium, and Magnesium - are among the nutrients most leached from crop soils by climate change. Until adequate nutrient replenishment of our soils can occur, or until climate change is reversed, we may need to rely on nutritional supplements to help protect our metabolism and prevent weight gain.

When cows, goats and sheep digest plants and grasses, they release the greenhouse gas methane; more methane is released from the animal's manure. As consumer demand for cow, goat, and sheep meat continues to increase, huge swaths of forestland and rainforest are cut down to create pastureland, releasing into the atmosphere another potent greenhouse gas-- the carbon dioxide stored in trees. Still another gas that impacts the atmosphere—nitrous oxide— gets released from the chemical fertilizers used on the crops that are grown to produce cattle feed. It doesn't take much thought to see how all of this interconnects in a web of toxicity.

Animal agriculture contributes an estimated 16.5 percent of total planetary greenhouse emissions, and environmental destruction from animal factories involves everything from the use of propane during production and the application of nitrogen fertilizers, to the gases emitted from mountains of animal manure. Dairy cattle produce the most pounds of greenhouse gases per animal per year (185 to 271 pounds) compared to swine at 10.5 pounds per animal per year. It's estimated that chickens produce 7 pounds of gases for every pound of chicken meat created. The larger the production facility and the more tightly these animals are crowded together, the more intense the release of these toxic gases.

Let's put the situation in simple dietary terms. "Beef requires 20 times more land and emits 20 times more greenhouse gas emissions per gram of edible protein than common plant proteins, such as beans," according to the World Resources Institute. Lamb is actually even more resource-intensive than beef.

Some well-meaning scientists recommend that people concerned about climate change simply replace beef with chicken in their dietary habits. Global consumers are responding by increasing chicken consumption by 31 percent in the first decade of the 21st century, compared to a 13 percent increase in beef consumption during the same period. But "swapping beef with chicken is akin to swapping a Hummer with a Ford F-150, not a Prius," pointed out Leah Garces, president of Mercy For Animals, and author of a book on the chicken industry. "When it comes to meat, the beef

"Climate Change." United States Department of Agriculture, Economic Research Service. https://www.ers.usda.gov/topics/natural-resources-environment/climate-change/
Karmaker R. Et al. "Potential Effects of Climate Change on Soil Properties: A Review." Science International. 2016. Chen Y. Et al. "Importance of Nutrients and Nutrient Metabolism on Human Health." Yale J Biol Med. 2018 June.
"Global Warming: How Does It Relate to Poultry?" Bulletin 1382. University of Georgia Extension. Department of Poultry Science. https://extension.uga.edu/
Publications 6 Pressing Questions About Beef and Climate Change, Answered." World Resources Institute. March 2022. https://www.wri.org/insights/6-pressing-questions-about- beef-and-climate-change-answered

industry is still the largest contributor to climate change. But the chicken industry is pretty bad, too. Its impact on the climate only looks benign when compared with beef."

Most of the nearly 10 billion chickens raised annually for meat in the United States live in warehouses longer than football fields, up to 10,000 of them stuffed into each building, enduring unimaginable suffering. Conditions in most other countries aren't much better. To feed these huge populations, the poultry industry (followed in severity by the pork industry) now utilizes most of the world's feed crops, an inefficient use of the planet's croplands, especially compared to the process of raising crops for direct human consumption. One serving of poultry at mealtime is a product of greenhouse gas emissions 11 times higher than what a comparable serving of a vegetable would be.

"So the next time someone recommends that we swap beef with chicken," wrote Leah Garces, "do them one better. Swap beef and chicken with more plants."

Two Stanford University professors—Patrick Brown, a biochemist, and geneticist Michael Eisen—created a model for phasing out animal agriculture over the next 15 years, an act which would provide 52 percent of the net emission reductions necessary to limit global warming to 2 degrees Celsius above pre-industrial levels. This is the minimum threshold most climate scientists say is required to avert worldwide disaster. Their model was published in a 2022 issue of the science journal, PLoS Climate, where they declared such a phaseout "represents our best and most immediate chance to reverse the trajectory of climate change."

They examined in detail four dietary scenarios for implementation by humanity to reduce greenhouse gas emissions: the first was an immediate replacement of all animal agriculture with a plant-based only diet; the second (and more realistic) option was a 15-year transition to a plant-diet globally; and the third and fourth options involved versions where only beef or beef and sheep were replaced with plant-only products, though neither option would make a sufficient dent in global warming.

"Animal agriculture contributes significantly to global warming through ongoing emissions of the potent greenhouse gases methane and nitrous oxide, and displacement of biomass carbon on the land used to support livestock," observed the two study authors, who quantified the cumulative negative effects on the atmosphere. "The magnitude and rapidity of these potential effects should place the reduction or elimination of animal agriculture at the forefront of strategies for averting disastrous climate change," they concluded.

"Replacing beef with chicken isn't as good for the planet as you think." Leah Garces. Vox. December 4, 2019. https://www.vox.com/future-perfect/2019/12/4/20993654/chicken-beef-climate-environment-factory-farms
"Why WWF Cares About Meat, Poultry, Dairy and Seafood." World Wildlife Fund. https://www.worldwildlife.org/pages/why-wwf-cares-about-meat-poultry-dairy-and-seafood "Replacing animal agriculture and shifting to a plant-based diet could drastically curb greenhouse gas emissions, according to the new model." Stanford University News. February 1, 2022. https://news.stanford.edu/2022/02/01/new-model-explores-link-animal-agriculture-climate-change/

The Humane Society International also strongly recommends "shifting to a plant-rich diet {as} one of the most effective climate-mitigation measures {that} provides multiple benefits from health and environmental perspectives. It is critically important for each of us to take action where we can, since we are all in this together."

Are most human beings too fixed in their eating habits for a partial or complete phaseout of animal agriculture to ever happen? Professor Brown answers by observing that history is replete with examples of mass changes in eating habits. "Five hundred years ago, nobody in Italy had ever seen a tomato. Sixty years ago, nobody in China had ever drunk a Coke. Mutton was once the most popular meat in America. People around the world readily adopt new foods, especially if they are delicious, nutritious, convenient and affordable." This book is our affirmation that the good professor is most certainly right.

Plant-based food options, as a viable dietary choice, represent a turning point opportunity for us as a species, a chance for us to alter the trajectory of both our individual and species health, as well as the environmental future of our planet. How often does that happen in one's personal life that a simple change in habits and attitude can have profound consequences beyond our own self?

The ultimate environmental protective diet is the Hippocrates Wellness living food program, particularly since it lowers energy needs and costs in the production and consumption of food.

By losing weight and keeping it off, using plants as one antidote to climate change, we seize the moral imperative to transform the sum total of our individual actions into a collective achievement that brings about planetary salvation.

Do it for yourself! Do it for others! Do it for the planet!

The choice is truly yours to make!

"Rapid global phaseout of animal agriculture has the potential to stabilize greenhouse gas levels for 30 years and offset 68 percent of CO2 emissions this century." Eisen MB. Brown PO. PLOS Climate. 2022 February.

"Animal Agriculture and Climate Change." Humane Society International. https://www.hsi.org/issues/climate-change/

Highlights

OF PART THREE

To develop healthy habits for weight loss, transform bad habits rather than suppress them; set weekly or even daily goals to do so, using positive thinking and affirmations.

Taking probiotic supplements can help to reinforce the beneficial bacteria in the stomach and gut that control nutrient absorption and resist the onset of obesity.

Experiment with dim lighting or even wearing a blindfold during meals to help limit your food intake; also eat from smaller plates, serve smaller portions, and always leave some food on your plate.

Distract yourself from food cravings by working puzzles or mental games, engage in a 'surf your urges' mindfulness practice, take a brisk walk or drink a large glass of water, use a 'tapping' technique, or eat spinach, peppers, and cinnamon. Preferably do a combination of these.

Use a visualization technique to gradually become the person you want to be by having a specific goal in mind and a picture or photo to focus on in meditation that represents your ideal body image.

Mind relaxation such as meditation and mindfulness exercises, have been shown in scientific studies to facilitate eating restraint and weight loss.

Behavioral change technology, like phone apps, help to support adherence to weight loss goals by tracking physical activity and eating habits.

Research indicates that hearing yourself crunch and chew food (while wearing white noise headphones), or counting the bites you take of each mouthful of food, helps to control food consumption.

Time your end-of-the-day meal for late afternoon, not at night, because studies show that late eaters gain more weight than early eaters. One reason being circadian rhythms – the body's internal biological clock – get disrupted by late eating.

Chronic stress releases cortisol which stimulates carbohydrate cravings
resulting in fat storage. Taking any or all of these herbs can provide stress relief:
a form of ginseng called Rhodiola, lemon balm, and ashwagandha root.

Regularly consume a pure organic combination of these proven fat fighting foods and
nutrients: marine green algae, Asian ginseng, ginger, chia seeds, avocado, sprouted nuts and
seeds, apples/pears, shiitake mushrooms, green tea, grapefruit, ashitaba, water and lemons.

A high-fiber plant-rich diet supports the growth of beneficial gut microbes that
help to keep your metabolism, immune system, and weight in balance.

To help reverse insulin resistance, a cause of weight gain, take brisk after-meal
walks, do weight training, and regularly immerse yourself in saunas and hot tubs.

Hormone replacement therapy for both men and women can reduce
abdominal fat and increase lean body mass in the long term.

Fat cell freezing can have a safe and effective impact, advancing weight loss,
but it isn't a substitute for healthy dieting and exercise.

Regular use of saunas and far-infrared saunas helps to trigger the body
to break up fat deposits, resulting in weight loss.

Taking short afternoon naps can help you to burn calories faster throughout the day.

People who take more than 8,000 steps a day are less likely
to become overweight, according to scientific evidence.

Studies show that morning exercise reduces abdominal fat
in women faster than exercise at other times of the day.

Create a weight loss and healthy weight management plan for yourself,
incorporating as many tips listed here as possible, in order to set in motion
a synergy that magnifies these overall health effects to your benefit.

Never lose sight of how our individual unhealthy food choices combine
to contribute to environmental degradation and accelerated climate change
Reliance on a plant-based organic diet can bring humans back from the
brink of planetary catastrophe. Your individual choices really do matter!

About the Authors

Brian Clement, Ph.D, NMD, LN, and his wife, **Anna Maria Clement, Ph.D, NMD, LN**, have spearheaded the international progressive health movement for more than five decades as Directors of the renowned Hippocrates Wellness (formerly known as the Hippocrates Health Institute), in West Palm Beach, Florida, the world's foremost complementary residential health center, which has served more than a half-million clients since its founding seven decades ago. Spa Magazine calls Hippocrates "the number one wellness spa in the world."

Over the last half-century, this couple and their team of healthcare professionals have pioneered clinical research and training in disease prevention, helping hundreds of thousands of participants who provided volumes of data, giving the Clements a privileged insight into the lifestyle required to prevent disease, enhance longevity, and maintain vitality. Their findings have provided the basis for the Hippocrates progressive, state-of-the-art treatments, and programs for health maintenance and recovery---their Life Transformation Program.

In addition to their research studies, the Clements conduct dozens of conferences before tens of thousands of people worldwide each year, educating on how to attain health and longevity, and giving humanity a roadmap for enriching our lives.

Individually and together, they have authored more than 20 books, including:

MAN-Opause: What Everyone Should Know About Treating Symptoms Of Male Hormone Imbalance, 2020, Rowman & Littlefield

Living Foods for Optimum Health, 1998, Harmony.

Hippocrates LifeForce, 2007, Healthy Living Publications. Cornell University nutritional biochemist Dr. Colin Campbell called this book, in his Preface to it, "One of the most important books ever written on nutrition."

Supplements Exposed, 2009, New Page Books.

7 Keys to Lifelong Sexual Vitality, 2012, New World Library.